Pissing on Demand

ALTERNATIVE CRIMINOLOGY SERIES
General Editor: Jeff Ferrell

PISSING ON DEMAND:
Workplace Drug Testing and the Rise of the Detox Industry
Kenneth D. Tunnell

Pissing on Demand

*Workplace Drug Testing and
the Rise of the Detox Industry*

Kenneth D. Tunnell

NEW YORK UNIVERSITY PRESS

New York and London

NEW YORK UNIVERSITY PRESS
New York and London
www.nyupress.org

Library of Congress Cataloging-in-Publication Data
Tunnell, Kenneth D.
Pissing on demand : workplace drug testing
and the rise of the detox industry / Kenneth D. Tunnell.
p. cm. — (Alternative criminolgy series)
Includes bibliographical references and index.
ISBN 0–8147–8280–9 (cloth : alk. paper) —
ISBN 0–8147–8281–7 (pbk : alk. paper)
1. Employees—Drug testing—United States. 2. Detoxification
(Substance abuse treatment)—United States. I. Title. II. Series.
HF5549.5.D7T86 2004
331.25'98—dc22   2003020502

New York University Press books are printed on acid-free paper,
and their binding materials are chosen for strength and durability.

Manufactured in the United States of America

c 10 9 8 7 6 5 4 3 2 1
p 10 9 8 7 6 5 4 3 2 1

Contents

Acknowledgments

Every book owes credit to someone and this one is no exception. Former graduate students Frank Wilson, Rob Sarver, and Colby Pitt worked as research assistants during the early stages of this work; research assistant Ryan Baker provided exceptional service in tracking down documents and case studies and in offering insights about the drug testing and resistance movements; my department chair, Carole Garrison, accommodated my teaching responsibilities and schedule to allow time to complete this manuscript; and Geil Geis and other reviewers offered constructive comments on earlier drafts of the manuscript. This work undoubtedly benefits from their critiques and kind encouragement.

I am especially grateful to Mark Hamm for his untold inspiration and friendship. Also thanks to Walter DeKeseredy for the late-night conversations over a few too many cans of cold Natural Ice. Thanks in particular to Jeff Ferrell, series editor, for ongoing interest in this work (even before he assumed editorship), inspiration, and comradery. I also am grateful to Stephen Magro and all the kind folks at New York University Press for enthusiastically supporting this work. Finally, I wish to thank White Oak Group/Burnham Inc. Publishers for giving me permission to include some material from the fourth chapter of my Burnham research monograph *Living Off Crime* (2000).

This book would have never gotten started without the body guard—Roscoe. Thanks for the tip.

Words are inadequate, but, once again, thank you Ilona for putting up with everything.

1

The Emergence of Drug Testing

Prologue

After a successful career with the U.S. Air Force, David Lee applies for a pilot's position with United Airlines. About the same time, his seventeen-year-old daughter, Hannah, applies for a part-time clerk's job with her local Walmart. Although qualifications and interview processes are vastly different for these two applicants, each has to comply with one similar corporate policy. Each must, in the presence of a witness, urinate into a specimen cup. For United and Walmart, this final step in the application process yields unequivocal validation of David's and Hannah's abilities to perform their respective duties, regardless of other qualifications that they may possess. And despite David's meritorious career as an air force pilot and Hannah's straight A high school performance and the fact that she is applying for only a part-time clerk's position, the urine sample has the ability to negate all other credentials. For if the sample test results are positive for drug use, each will be denied employment and perhaps forbidden from ever again applying to those corporations.

David's and Hannah's stories often are lost in the political maze of drug-testing policies and procedures. Yet, they are hardly unique, as millions of workers now face similar scrutiny. Pissing on demand is now a widely accepted requirement for employment. In the midst of these new invasive procedures for determining credentials, some job applicants and employees decide to quietly engage in subterfuge. This is their story.

During the past two decades, Americans have witnessed some frightening social and political changes governing drug use. The U.S. government initiated an international war on drugs; a national drug czar was appointed and a White House Office on Drug Abuse created; public expenditures for the war on drugs increased exponentially, from $1.5 billion in 1981

1

to $19.2 billion for 2003—a 1200 percent increase ("Drug free work-place" 2002), with most of the monies (viz., 67 percent) earmarked for activities other than drug rehabilitation; "Just Say No" and "DARE to Say No to Drugs" became public strategies for reducing drug use; zero tolerance became a stated goal and a popular-culture expression; asset forfeiture laws were passed whereby law enforcement could, with impunity, seize properties of those merely suspected of using them for, or acquiring them from, drug trafficking, thereby shifting the burden of proof to the accused; federal policies were created and upheld in a U.S. Supreme Court ruling in March 2002 whereby residents of public housing are evicted for possessing or using drugs on the premises; the issuance of "no-knock" warrants, which allow authorities to simply run through suspects' doors, became more commonplace; stop and frisk procedures, within the context of the further erosion of search and seizure laws, became an accepted component of order maintenance policing; the use of the military in international and domestic campaigns to contain drug use became commonplace; mandatory prison sentences increased (in some cases to life sentences) for drug possession and trafficking with the result that the number of individuals incarcerated for drug offenses increased from 431,291 in 1992 to 625,358 in 1999—a 45 percent increase (*Economic Costs of Drug Abuse in the United States* 2001); and the even newer war on terrorism (since September 11, 2001) has dovetailed with the war on drugs, with the newly created White House Office of Homeland Security and the White House drug czar (along with the Pentagon) coordinating efforts.

But, drug users and traffickers, or those typically regarded as criminal problem populations, are far from the only ones suspected of deviance and subjected to these forms of increasing surveillance. Policymakers eventually turned their attention to suspected drug users who, it was alleged, are harmful to business, the national economy, and a general quality of life. These other drug users who increasingly have come under suspicion and monitoring are otherwise law-abiding, working, and tax-paying men and women.

As containment efforts shifted to this new population of deviants, an abundance of news coverage and political rhetoric emerged about the many adverse consequences of drug use in the workplace. Claims have been made that workplace drug use adversely affects industry, public health, and the national economy in extraordinary ways. The Office of National Drug Control Policy (NDCP) tracks public costs of drug abuse in the categories of health care, productivity, and other miscellaneous areas. According to NDCP reports, during the 1990s, the overall cost of drug abuse increased 5.9 percent annually from $102.2 billion in 1992 to a total societal cost of $160.7 billion in 2000. Of the three categories, productivity losses comprise the bulk, at 69 percent of total losses. For example, in 1992, productivity losses were placed at $69.4 billion; in 2000 such losses reached the $110.5 billion mark. By comparison, health-care costs were at $14.9 billion for 2000 (*Economic Costs of Drug Abuse in the United States* 2001).

Although such figures are broadly propagated, these and more recent numbers are widely disputed, partly because of the difficulty of measuring losses in productivity and profits that result from one single issue or problem (e.g., workplace drug or alcohol use). Teasing out such estimates is undoubtedly complex; results arguably are less than definitive and yearly estimates vary widely. Nonetheless, published research methodologies used for collecting these data are based on sound and widely accepted scientific procedures. In response to such overwhelming evidence of increased societal costs from drug abuse, the past two decades witnessed the meteoric rise of antidrug-use policies both general and workplace related. Such policies are manifest in a variety of activities, including the testing of job applicants and current employees for drug use. Measuring workplace drug use with data acquired from testing applicants and employees initially revealed fairly high levels of drug use. Over time, they have declined. But, as most critics of drug-testing policies and procedures continually remind us, testing, as currently performed, reveals previous rather than current use, which is the stated concern among drug-testing proponents.

Early in the public and private campaigns for corporate drug-testing programs, companies often were given the news that drug use costs business $33 billion each year in lost productivity. This figure originated from a 1984 Research Triangle study that actually never examined lost productivity resulting from drug use. Rather, the research simply compared wage differentials between marijuana-using households and nonusing ones. Increases in the original figure across the next few years were simply based on adjustments for inflation (Morgan 1988). A decade before the Research Triangle study, during a 1972 Firestone Corporation luncheon, a speaker encouraged the company, in order to reduce costs associated with alcohol abuse, to adopt an employee assistance program as a cost-effective policy. The focus was on "medical-behavioral problems," specifically alcohol-related ones. The speaker and the source of the data remain publicly unidentified to this day although the report (minus the original data) was published a year later. Ten years afterwards, the information from the report was reproduced in the *Drug Abuse and Alcoholism Newsletter.* Data from the original source were defended as scientific and methodologically sound. Furthermore, they were misrepresented as reflecting illicit drug use and as representative of industry in general (Cohen 1983; cf. Gilliom 1994: 40). The misinformation was reproduced many times over in drug testing corporations' promotional literature, in anti-drug-use advertising, by politicians, and in the mainstream press. The National Academy of Sciences' commentary on the report and its use claims that "the data . . . do not provide clear evidence of the deleterious effects of drugs other than alcohol on safety and other job performance indicators" (Normand, Lempert, and O'Brien 1994a: 107). Nonetheless, the report, with its misinterpreted data, became reified as it took on a life of its own and evolved into another justification for companies' efforts at implementing drug-testing programs (*Drug Testing: A Bad Investment* 1999). Given this report and the ongoing estimates of losses from employee drug use, it is hardly surprising that informed and scientifically grounded research was lost or buried in a race for a solution to a somewhat misinformed public and a socially constructed drug problem.

Employers implemented drug testing after having become convinced that testing programs would reduce costs resulting from employee absenteeism, accidents, and theft, each of which is assumed to result from employee drug use. Technological determinism also has been credited with the rise of drug testing. As the technology for testing large groups of workers became accessible, so too did the assumption that testing was necessary to stem the tide of workplace drug abuse (Gilliom 1994: 36). Companies implemented testing policies so quickly and at such a volume that one could surmise that they evidently defined drug testing as a panacea. Yet, during the late 1980s, when companies were adopting drug-testing programs wholesale, there was little scientific evidence available about the validity of the costs associated with employee drug use. Corporations were left to the information provided them by parties that oftentimes had vested interests in implementing drug-testing programs. Companies within the drug-testing industry itself glorified the benefits of testing employees. Drug testing was also promoted by the federal government as it persuaded employers to join the national war on drugs. Federal and state governments began offering corporations all sorts of financial and legal incentives for participating in this facet of the war on drugs (Zimmer and Jacobs 1992). Today, the drug-testing enterprise is a multibillion-dollar industry.

Workplace anti-drug-use strategies also initially were fueled by disparate and (fortunately few) tragic workplace events in which workers were later determined to have been under the influence of one drug or another. For example, after an Amtrak train wreck, engineers were discovered to have been under the influence of marijuana; in another case a national bank's computer system collapsed, allegedly because of programmers' drug use. Although tragic and costly, these events offer little information about the pervasiveness of workplace drug use or its associated and real costs. In actuality, the "extent of drug use on the job, much less drug-related losses, is not known" and has never been known (Nock 1993: 100; cf. Shepard and Clifton 1998). Nonetheless, lost revenue and workplace safety are the most common reasons given by employers supporting drug testing.

Only in recent history has workplace drug use been defined as a social problem by social scientists, medical experts, and employers. The Shafer Commission of 1972 (a blue ribbon panel of presidential appointees), the Domestic Council on Drug Abuse Task Force of 1975 assembled by President Ford, and the Liaison Task Force Panel of 1978 appointed by President Carter each investigated and reported that drug use, and cocaine use in particular, was a rather insignificant social problem. Yet, just a few short years afterwards such interpretations of drug use seemingly were disregarded, although workplace drug use and abuse apparently had changed little. Indeed, drug use generally changed little, except for a decreasing trend. Data indicate that general drug use declined from 25 percent of young adults reporting current use (i.e., within the previous month) in 1985 to a low of 13 percent in 1992. Since then the trend shows a slight increase to 18 percent in 2000 (*National Household Survey on Drug Abuse* 2001). The percentage of persons reporting current drug use decreased consistently and across all age categories from the high point of 1979 to 1992 (*National Household Survey on Drug Abuse* 1997; Mieczkowski 1996). In other words, "there was no nationwide burst in drug use in the 1980s that can account for the eruption of attention and action in the circles of media, government, and public opinion" (Gilliom 1994: 22; *Economic Costs of Alcohol and Drug Abuse in the United States* 1992). Policies based on concerns about drug abuse, however, were not entirely misplaced or without justification. While reported drug use decreased markedly during the second half of the 1980s (the decade during which the bulk of drug-testing policies were enacted), use has increased since then. Current levels remain below those of the late 1970s and early 1980s. Data show, for example, in 1996 an estimated 13 million Americans (6.1 percent of the population over age twelve) were current users of illicit drugs. In 2000, an estimated 14 million Americans (6.3 percent of the population over age twelve) were current users of illicit drugs. Although drug use is higher among the unemployed, most drug users are employed. Indeed, of the 11.8 million adult drug users in 2000, 9.1 million, or 77 percent, were employed (*National Household Survey on Drug Abuse* 1997, 2001). Due in part to these data (and the social construction of a workplace drug-use problem), drug testing in the workplace became the normative method for screening applicants and routinely investigating employees.

Given the degree to which drug testing entered the workplace and pre-employment application processes, the casual observer probably would assume that workplace drug use represents a critical social problem affecting economic growth, safety, employees' loyalty and reliability, and costs to employers, consumers, and taxpayers. Evidence to date from employers themselves disputes assumptions that workplace drug use is a major social problem. For example, a survey conducted during the early 1990s found that 0.3 percent of employers defined drugs in the workplace as a major problem although an additional 8 percent considered it a moderate one (Zeese 1997: 1.1). Evidence indicates that the driving impetus for drug testing has not come from employers but rather from "public anxiety about drug use, aggressive marketing by drug testing companies, and government regulations and policies requiring testing" (Zeese 1997: 1.2). Today about 40 percent of Fortune 500 companies conduct drug screening but most report that they test employees because they are required to rather than because they believe drug use in the workplace is a significant problem. Acceptance of drug-testing policies and increased use of drug testing, by most accounts, probably is a response to government initiatives rather than to a worsening and empirically observable social problem.

Testing is not limited to Fortune 500 corporations. With the kickoff of the "Drugs Don't Work" campaign of President George Bush Sr., the federal government turned its attention to small businesses with the intention of persuading them to test their employees. Although at that time 85 percent of small-business owners reported that drug use was not a significant problem, today businesses of every size in the industrial and service sectors have implemented applicant and employee drug-testing policies (Zeese 1997). This change resulted in part from the 15 percent of small-business owners reporting drug use as a significant problem. It also is attributed to the wider issues of shifting public opinion about drug use and government initiatives to business for implementing testing programs.

Drug-testing results confirm employers' perceptions of the pervasiveness of drug use in the workplace. During the late 1980s, overall positive findings were 13.6 percent. Since 1988, positive results have steadily declined to 4.7 percent in 1999. Among safety-sensitive positions, positive findings were at 3.2 percent in 1999 (*Drug Testing Index* 1999). Between 1 and 3 percent of employees subjected to random testing have tested positive for drug use.[1] Likewise, SmithKline Beecham Clinical Laboratories (a major player in the testing industry) reports that overall positive findings have decreased from 18 percent in 1987 to 6 percent in 1996. These data complement those of the semiannual *Drug Testing Index,* which shows that positive results decreased from a high of 13.6 percent in 1988 to a low of 4.7 percent for 1999 ("Drug abuse and workplace demographics" 2001). Although screening proponents claim that testing initiatives themselves have affected employee drug use, inferring a causal relationship at this point is premature. There may be other valid explanations for these declining positive results. For example, age-related decreases in drug use, the informal pressures to desist, the overall declining rates of drug use since the late 1970s, individuals' discovery and use of detox products, and other methods of subverting testing procedures (detox and subversion are addressed later in this book) are equally credible explanations. Furthermore, the American Management Association claims that early workplace drug screening commonly focused on workers "suspected" of drug use. As the screening net widened to include workers who were not suspected of use, increasing numbers of nonusers were tested. This also probably has contributed to decreasing trends in positive results ("Supreme Court v. teens 2002").

According to the most recent household survey of 2000, nearly 77 percent of adults who reported current illicit drug use (as measured by use within the previous thirty days) are employed either full or part time. This percentage translates into 9.1 million people or 6.4 percent of the nation's adult work force ("Drug abuse and workplace demographics" 2001; *National Household Survey on Drug Abuse* 2001). Of those individuals testing positive for drug use, there is no evidence that they were under the influence while at work. (Indeed, only blood testing, which is rarely used, can detect impairment from alcohol and drugs, and only the Breathalyzer, which is not used by employers, can determine alcohol intoxication.) This is especially the case with marijuana, the drug found most often through testing (about 40 percent of positive results indicate marijuana use). Marijuana continues to be the illicit drug of choice among Americans. It reportedly is used by 77 percent of all illicit drug users, or about 10.1 million Americans (*National Household Survey on Drug Abuse* 1997), although new marijuana users declined from 2.6 million in 1996 to 2.0 million in 1999 (*National Household Survey on Drug Abuse* 2001). Marijuana metabolites,[2] unlike, say, cocaine, typically are detectable in chronic users' urine sometimes weeks after their last use of the drug. As a result of tests' inability to differentiate impairment from previous use, the American Medical Association has called for the development of more sophisticated technologies that are able to distinguish between the two. To date, there has been little political will for creating and implementing such discerning testing measures, which suggests that the actual purpose of workplace drug testing is to control drug use generally rather than workplace drug use in particular.

Accidents in the workplace are more likely to be related to fatigue, stress, and illness than to external factors (including drug use). Among those worst-case accidents involving a worker's death, alcohol is the drug most commonly detected. Yet drug-testing programs rarely include screening for the presence of alcohol (other than in cases where testing is done "for cause" or in postaccident instances). Indeed, drug screening programs are more than twice as likely to test for illicit drugs as for alcohol although the latter is associated with far more on-site accidents, absenteeism, tardiness, and overall poor job performance. In American society, alcohol remains the drug of choice and abuse, whether on or off the job.

Proponents of drug-testing initiatives typically speak in terms of dollars and cents, that is, the amount of money drug use costs because of work-related accidents and lost productivity. The claim is made that testing programs have the ability to counter such public expense, a questionable conjecture since testing programs continue to screen for illicit drugs rather than the costliest drug of abuse—alcohol—or the other costly yet legal and highly addictive drug—tobacco. According to the *National Household Survey on Drug Abuse, 2000* (2001), 46.6 percent, or 104 million Americans, currently drink alcohol. About 29.3 percent, or 65.5

million Americans, reportedly are current users of tobacco products. These figures obviously far surpass those on illicit drug use.

The National Institute on Drug Abuse has estimated an annual cost to industry from alcohol abuse in excess of $67 billion (Ackerman 1991: 19). These data, however, like costs attributed to drug use, are equally murky, especially when one compares them to other estimates of alcohol-related costs. For example, estimates from 1992 place total alcohol costs (including industrial, health, and social expenses) at $148 billion and estimates from 1998 place those costs at $184 billion (Harwood 2000; Harwood, Fountain, and Livermore 1998). Costs to industry alone are estimated at $134 billion for 1998 (Harwood 2000) or about 2.3 percent of the gross national product. Data indicate that alcohol costs are not attributed solely to alcoholics or "problem drinkers." Hangovers among modest drinkers allegedly cost the U.S. workplace about $148 billion annually in absenteeism and poor job performance, an average of two thousand dollars per working adult (Wiese, Shlipak, and Browner 2000). The National Institute on Alcohol Abuse and Alcoholism estimated that alcohol abuse in the United States cost $166 billion in 1995—a 12 percent increase since 1992. About 60 percent of those costs from alcohol abuse are workplace related. All these data show that alcohol abuse and its related costs evidently are increasing. These data indicate too that alcohol use also allegedly is a significant social problem yet currently is of little concern to testing advocates, especially when compared to illicit drug use. But, these data on alcohol must be considered with caution, just as with figures on drug use. It remains difficult to tease out actual costs from one factor, whether it be alcohol, drugs, fatigue, or some other cause. Despite well-intended research, the picture remains murky.

Fourth and Fifth Amendment Issues

For a time, the most significant constitutional issue facing employee drug-testing programs was the Fourth Amendment protection against the government's unreasonable search and seizure. However, what once may have appeared as a constitutional safeguard against intrusions into one's private affairs today is diminished due to a combination of both criminal and drug-testing court decisions (Zeese 1997: 1.28). Regarding drug testing, courts generally have measured individuals' expectations of privacy against public safety and security. Given this duality, in drug-testing cases it has been difficult for individuals' personal rights to prevail. Privacy, a recognized fundamental value within American society, is not mentioned in the United States Constitution although the Supreme Court, in key rulings of the 1960s and 1970s, did assert that the right to privacy is implicit in the Bill of Rights (e.g., *Griswold v. Connecticut* and *Roe v. Wade*; Gilliom 1994: chapter 5). The principles applied in those cases, which were limited mostly to sexuality and decisions about pregnancy, have not been applied to drug-testing cases. Most challenges to drug testing have relied on issues of privacy and unreasonable searches. Although the Fourth Amendment protects against "unreasonable" searches and seizures, drug testing has been deemed as reasonable.

Gilliom's (1994: 86) assessment of courts' logic is instructive, for it places decisions that effectively weakened Fourth Amendment safeguards within a social-historical explanation. For example, courts have placed drug tests

> in the category of "administrative searches" that meet "special needs" of the government relating to safety, security or workplace management. Then by "balancing" the rights of the individual against the needs of the government, it is ruled that the drug-testing programs . . . are not unreasonable searches.

In other words, courts have largely reclassified "criminal policies as administrative" and have "coloniz[ed] the workplace as a site of surveillance and control" by extending the net and thinning the mesh of social control (Gilliom 1994: 119; Cohen 1985: 42).

Two distinct cases have had the greatest impact on Fourth Amendment issues regarding drug testing. During 1985, the Federal Railroad Administration, in response to its findings that "between 1972 and 1983 drug- or alcohol-related train accidents killed forty-two people, injured sixty-one and cost $19 million in property damage," passed new policies that required employee drug testing in postaccident situations, for reasonable suspicion and in cases in which employees hold sensitive positions (West and Ackerman 1993: 584). At the same time, the U.S. Customs Service began subjecting employees seeking promotion or transfer to drug tests as part of physical exams (which are a condition of employment). In the face of these developments, railroad workers and federal agents filed separate suits that eventually were heard by the United States Supreme Court.

The Supreme Court in 1989 upheld a California district court and reversed the court of appeals by ruling that railroad workers can be subject to random drug testing, which, according to the Court's logic, does not violate Fourth Amendment restrictions on unreasonable searches and seizures (*Samuel K. Skinner v. Railway Labor Executives' Association et al.*). The ruling affected public employees working for federal, state, county, and municipal governments. Private employees were unaffected by the ruling. They, unlike public-sector workers, have no constitutional protection from searches and seizures from their private- (rather than public-) sector employers. Writing for the majority, Justice Anthony Kennedy also upheld the use of the Enzyme Mediated Immunoassay Technique (EMIT) and the Gas Chromatography/Mass Spectrometry (GC/MS) drug-testing procedures (the most commonly used), claiming that they are "highly accurate." (EMIT and GC/MS are described in the following chapter.)

On the same day as the *Skinner* ruling, the Court, in a 5-4 decision in *National Treasury Employees Union v. Von Raab,* held that Customs Service agents, like railroad workers, can be subjected to drug testing and that such procedures do not violate Fourth Amendment protections. The Court, as in *Skinner,* balanced the necessity of agents having unimpeachable integrity with the needs of the government and of society, as well as with public safety concerns. Due to their jobs and the intrusions on their privacy that were already in place, the Court ruled that railroad workers and customs agents have diminished expectations of privacy. These rulings were based on the logic that "drug testing is necessary to preserve public health and safety, national security, or government integrity." As long as employers' testing programs are accurate and reasonably sensitive to employee privacy, courts generally have upheld them (Tulacz and O'-Toole 1991: 44).

Writing for the minority in the *Von Raab* case, Justice Scalia stated that even "school crossing guards" would be subject to drug testing under this ruling. And indeed, only six years later, in 1995, in *Vernonia School District 47J v. Acton,* the Court upheld the testing of junior-high-school student-athletes, citing the fact that reasonable suspicion existed that student-athletes were both using and promoting drug use (Zeese 1997: 1.34). Then, in June 2002, in a 5-4 decision, the United States Supreme Court, in *Board of Pottawatomie County et al. v. Lindsay Earls et al.,* upheld a drug-testing program in Tecumseh, Oklahoma, that forced students to piss on demand if they participated in any extracurricular activities (including the school choir, marching band, and the academic team, in each of which plaintiff Lindsay Earls took part). Tecumseh's program tests students at the beginning of the school year and then randomly throughout the year. Positive findings or refusal to submit to testing results in expulsion from extracurricular activities for the remainder of the academic year.

Since 1989, federal circuit courts generally have relied on the *Skinner* ruling when upholding drug testing. Courts likewise have ruled that pre-employment drug testing of applicants does not violate Fourth and Fifth Amendment guarantees.

Although they depart from Supreme Court decisions of three decades ago, the Court's rulings on drug testing have remained fairly consistent. In 1997, for example, the Court overturned a Georgia ruling that allowed drug testing of individuals currently holding or seeking public office. Given that drug testing is considered a search within the meaning of the Fourth and Fourteenth Amendments, Supreme Court Justice Ruth Bader Ginsberg, writing for the majority, concluded that testing is limited to those cases in which a reasonable suspicion exists or in special-needs cases such as transportation workers, soldiers, and law enforcement officers. The Court noted that a special need "must be substantial—important enough to override the individual's acknowledged privacy interest" (*Chandler v. Miller*). As a result, those holding and those seeking public office are exempt from testing.

The Fifth Amendment protects individuals from being compelled to testify against themselves. Arguments are that public-sector employers violate employees' Fifth Amendment rights by subjecting them to drug testing, the results of which may be incriminating. Courts, however, have sided with drug-testing public employers over employees on two grounds. First, courts have ruled that the Fifth Amendment is limited to the government compelling individuals to *testify* against themselves. As a result, requiring physical evidence such as blood, urine, and hair samples rather than testimony from individuals is not a violation of their Fifth Amendment guarantees. Second, courts have ruled that the Fifth Amendment protects individuals from self-incrimination in *criminal proceedings*—rulings that exclude drug-testing policies, which are regarded as personnel matters (Tulacz and O'Toole 1991: 45). As a result, public and private employers are legally allowed to require applicant and employee drug screening.

Executive and Legislative Actions

During the twentieth century, various political efforts were made to contain the availability and use of illicit drugs. The last decade or so of the nineteenth century witnessed the emergence of a few state laws aimed at controlling drug use, and in 1887 federal law banned the importation of opium (Lyman and Potter 1996: chapter 1). In 1906, Congress passed the Pure Food and Drug Act, which required warning labels for addictive pharmaceuticals although the law did little to restrict the use of these drugs. Opiate use effectively was criminalized with the passage of the Harrison Narcotics Act of 1914. The act required specific restrictions on prescription drugs (e.g., prescription record maintenance) and required individuals prescribing or distributing drugs to both register with the Treasury Department and purchase government tax stamps. Those failing to comply were considered unlawful drug traffickers (Ackerman 1991; Lyman and Potter 1996: chapter 1).

In 1919, the Eighteenth Amendment was ratified, prohibiting alcohol manufacturing, sale, and use. Although numerous containment laws were passed, marijuana remained legal. In fact, it was prescribed for various medical problems until the Marijuana Tax Act of 1937, which proclaimed marijuana a gateway drug and dangerous narcotic. During the 1950s, two laws, the Boggs Act and the Narcotics Control Act, increased penalties for marijuana and other narcotics trafficking. In 1965 the Drug Abuse Control Amendments were passed; they created criminal penalties for illegally manufacturing the increasingly popular drugs—amphetamines and barbiturates (Lyman and Potter 1996: chapter 1). Then, in 1971, Congress passed the toughest antidrug legislation to date, the Controlled Substances Act, which superseded both the Harrison and the Narcotic Control Acts. The Controlled Substances Act, however, primarily targeted the abuse of pharmaceuticals, leaving drugs produced in underground economies relatively untouched (Ackerman 1991). Then, in a somewhat progressive bill, Congress passed the Federal Rehabilitation Act of 1973, which prohibited federal agencies and any recipient of federal financial assistance from discriminating against qualified handicapped persons. The progressive component of this move was that according to the act, alcoholics and drug addicts were considered handicapped persons unless their drug or alcohol use interfered with successful fulfillment of job performance expectations or their behavior threatened others' safety or property. Although the Federal Rehabilitation Act allowed employers to require both job applicants and employees to submit to drug and alcohol testing as part of comprehensive physical examinations, "the question of whether employers could [have] discharge[d] or refuse[d] to hire an individual solely on the basis of a positive test result . . . [was] unresolved" (Fay 1991: 23). The Rehabilitation Act was revised in 1978 to exclude from protection those individuals with alcohol or drug addictions unless their addictions did not threaten the safety of persons or property. The revisions provided for increased employer subjectivity in making decisions about employees' addictions and the extent to which they threaten persons and property.

The next section will describe more recent changes in drug-testing policies and procedures. First, however, the following developments are pertinent for a social and historical understanding of the current state of drug testing in the United States:

- During the 1960s and 1970s, the Department of Defense began performing urinalyses on military personnel returning home from combat in Vietnam. Indeed, a negative test result was required before personnel could actually leave Vietnam. Although extreme, these measures resulted from widespread reports that 10 to 25 percent of GIs were addicted to heroin. The reports were repudiated when testing produced positive results of 4.5 percent (Massing 1998: 107, 115). Nonetheless, testing, as policy, remained.
- In 1972, the Syva Company developed a reliable and inexpensive technology for detecting marijuana. The new test, Enzyme-Mediated Immunoassay Test (EMIT), was marketed as a portable kit for on-site testing.
- This new technology coincided with the Defense Department's survey research, which revealed high levels of drug use among military personnel while on and off the job. A worldwide self-report survey of U.S. military personnel showed that 26 percent of respondents had used marijuana within the previous thirty days; 10 percent reported having used more than one illicit drug and 21 percent claimed that drug use had affected their work. Shortly afterwards, a congressionally authorized survey indicated that more than 50 percent of navy personnel reported using marijuana at least weekly and 29 percent claimed to have used cocaine; 42.3 percent claimed

to have used drugs or alcohol (or to have been under their influence) while on the job (Walsh and Trumble 1991: 27).

- In May 1981, several crew members accidentally were killed while serving aboard the *U.S.S. Nimitz*. Postmortem toxicology results indicated the presence of illegal drugs.
- During February 1982, the U.S. Navy initiated worldwide programs for on-site drug testing of all its personnel.
- In 1982, utility and transportation directors began discussions of drug use among their employees, which culminated in a task force representing the electric, gas, and nuclear industries.
- In 1983, the Greyhound Corporation began testing its bus drivers. This screening initiative was welcome news to other transportation companies, who were awaiting such developments before initiating their testing programs.
- During the early and mid-1980s, startling revelations, surveys, and high-profile drug-related events became headline news and the subject of television coverage. The accidental overdose deaths of college basketball star Len Bias and the National Football League's Don Rogers (in 1986) and subsequent media attention fanned the flames of antidrug rhetoric and action. These mediated images undoubtedly played a powerful part in reifying the drug problem; the public was becoming convinced of an escalating drug problem in the United States and in the workplace. There was much to consider. For example, a 1983 story described a national transportation safety report claiming that seven train wrecks within a single year involved alcohol or drugs; another story highlighted Triangle Park researchers' estimates that drug abuse cost society $25.8 billion in 1983; *Newsweek* claimed that illegal drug use in the workplace had become "a crisis for American business" (Walsh and Trumble 1991: 28). By the end of 1983, various companies had implemented employee drug-testing programs.
- Labor unions, beginning with the Teamsters Union and Transit Workers Union, under pressure to concede to industry, began renegotiating contracts that allowed for employee drug testing.
- The International Olympic Committee began discussions about testing competitors during the 1984 games.
- By 1985, drug testing in the workplace had become commonplace among large corporations (e.g., General Motors and Exxon) and

by August, 25 percent of Fortune 500 companies were testing job applicants.

- In 1985, the Defense Department established drug-testing procedures for its civilian employees.
- A New Jersey hospital's employee survey results, which were widely discussed in the media, reported the fantastic news that 75 percent of respondents claimed to have used illegal drugs while on the job and 64 percent reported that drugs interfered with their job performance (Walsh and Trumble 1991).
- By 1986, midsize private-sector employers were testing employees and applicants at a rapidly growing pace.
- The public became further convinced. In 1986, public polls indicated that Americans supported drug-testing initiatives. In fact, 77 percent said they would not object to being tested; 62 percent supported mandatory testing for federal employees; and 43 percent supported testing in the private sector. Another poll indicated that 75 percent of full-time workers were willing to subject themselves to drug testing and would not consider it an invasion of privacy (Walsh and Trumble 1991: 36).
- By 1986, the drug-testing industry was growing at a rate of 10 percent annually, yielding increasing profits for manufacturing and testing firms.

Given these events, it hardly is surprising that government and business officials defined the situation as dire. As a result, in March 1986, the President's Commission on Organized Crime made the sweeping recommendation that all employees of private companies under contract with the federal government be "regularly subjected to urine testing for drugs as a condition of employment" (Ackerman 1991: 10). On September 15, 1986, former President Ronald Reagan issued his Executive Order 12564: Drug-Free Federal Workplace, which was effective immediately. Raising the battle flag of the war on drugs, Reagan's manifesto claimed,

Drug use is having serious adverse effects upon a significant proportion of the national work force and results in billions of dollars of lost productivity each year. . . . Federal employees who use illegal drugs, on or off duty, tend to be less productive, less reliable, and prone to greater absenteeism than their fellow employees who do not use illegal drugs. The use of illegal drugs, on or off duty, by Federal employees impairs the efficiency of Federal departments and agencies, undermines public confidence in them, and makes it more difficult for other employees who do not use illegal drugs to perform their jobs effectively. The use of illegal drugs, on or off duty, by Federal employees also can pose a serious health and safety threat to members of the public and to other Federal employees.

Recognizing that the federal government is the country's single largest employer, Reagan claimed that he wanted a program "designed to offer drug users a helping hand," although just a few short paragraphs later he stated that "persons who use illegal drugs are not suitable for Federal employment." His order provided for "identifying illegal drug users, including testing," and authorized "the head of each Executive agency to test any applicant for illegal drug use." This order called for mandatory random testing programs in "all agencies of the Executive Branch." That same day, in his "Message to Congress Transmitting Proposed Legislation," he "pledged to make the fight against drug abuse one of [his] highest priorities," citing as evidence of his commitment the fact that in less than five years, "our spending for drug law enforcement has nearly tripled." Congress supported Reagan's initiative and passed the Supplemental Appropriations Act for Fiscal Year 1987, which "required the U.S. Department of Health and Human Services to issue mandatory guidelines to govern the implementation" of Executive Order 12564 and to establish testing programs among the various agencies of the federal government (Drug-Free Federal Workplace 1986; Tulacz and O'Toole 1991: 14; Ackerman 1991: 10).

The broadest action for private employees was the passage of the Drug-Free Workplace Act of 1988 (Public Law 100-690, Nov. 18, 1988), which requires employers with federal contracts worth at least one hundred thousand dollars and any recipient of a federal grant to institute a comprehensive drug-free workplace program. Although the act was far reaching and was touted as comprehensive, nothing in it required employers to test employees or applicants; neither were employers required to provide employees with assistance or rehabilitation. Afterwards, the Department of Defense, the Department of Transportation, the Federal Highway Administration, the Federal Aviation Administration, the United States Coast Guard, the Urban Mass Transportation Administration, and the Nuclear Regulatory Commission implemented their own drug-free workplace policies authorizing drug testing of applicants and employees at various junctures (e.g., preemployment, random, rehabilitation, etc.).

On October 28, 1991, President George Bush Sr. signed the Omnibus Transportation Employee Testing Act of 1991 (Public Law 102-143, Oct. 28, 1991) stipulating testing employees within the Federal Aviation Administration, the Federal Highway Administration, the Federal Railroad Administration, and the Urban Mass Transportation Administration. The act, among other things, added alcohol to the list of drugs for testing. This act preempted state laws and authorized both random and preemployment drug and alcohol testing. Similar policies as mandated by the Omnibus Transportation Employee Testing Act are now in place for the Department of Defense, the Nuclear Regulatory Commission, the Department of Energy, and the National Aeronautical and Space Administration.[3]

The Reagan and Bush administrations denied any distinction between soft and hard drugs and casual and chronic drug users. Prior to their administrations, federal drug policies were politically more progressive. The Nixon administration, which initiated one of the country's first wars on drugs, nonetheless valued and funded rehabilitation and treatment as reasonable policies (along with law enforcement) for addressing the dysfunctions of drug abuse. In fact, Nixon earmarked 68 percent of his drug-war budget for treatment and rehabilitation of addicts (Massing 1998: chapter 8). By 1973, a year into Nixon's second term, federal spending on treatment and prevention totaled $420 million, "more than eight times the amount when Nixon took office" (Massing 1998: 119). The Ford administration followed suit. The Carter administration actually advocated the decriminalization of marijuana and budgeted large amounts of monies to education and treatment for hard-core users (Massing 1998).

The drug war escalated exponentially under the Reagan and Bush administrations with increasing monies being allocated for attacking the supply side and for interdiction at the nation's borders. In fact, the Reagan administration scaled back the money for treatment by 25 percent. "Taking into account the inflation-driven declines of the Carter years, this amounted to a 43 percent reduction in federal treatment funds in just a few years. In real terms, federal spending on treatment was less than one-fourth what it had been in 1974" (Massing 1998: 161). By 1986, two years into Reagan's second term, "80 percent of the $2.2 billion drug budget was going for the supply side, compared to just 20 percent for the demand side—the reverse of the ratio during the Nixon years" (Massing 1998: 180).

Since the initiatives of the Reagan and Bush administrations, which many observers originally considered anomalies, former President Clinton continued the war on drugs by advocating drug-testing programs and by funding law enforcement initiatives at expenditure levels far beyond those of his predecessors. Although originally committed to treatment and to advancing demand-side policies, Clinton "waffled" in the face of new data indicating marijuana use was up among American teenagers (Massing 1998: chapter 16). The Clinton administration, unfortunately late in its tenure, through an executive order, directed the Federal Employees Health Benefit Program, the nation's largest health-insurance plan, to provide full coverage for substance abuse treatment and to consider it equal to any other medical condition ("Drug abuse and workplace demographics" 2001). To date, there is no indication from the George Bush Jr. administration that it will recommend any significant changes in drug-testing policies or the general war on drugs. Public expenditures for the war on drugs and the number of battle strategies have steadily increased regardless of president or political party in power. Testing, as a means of social control and as one component of the war on drugs, likewise has expanded unabatedly.

Workplace drug testing has not taken hold internationally as it has in the United States. One significant exception is in transportation. Beginning in July 1997, all motor carriers in other countries were required to comply with the drug-testing requirements of transportation workers based in the United States. The United States and Mexico signed an agreement in 1998 under which Mexico will initiate a testing program that parallels those in the United States for commercial transportation drivers who enter the United States. Likewise, the United States's regulations will impact Canadian transportation workers who enter the United States. In Canada, there currently are no laws that prohibit workplace drug testing for transportation workers. A professional organization—the European Workplace Drug Testing Society—has as its mission professionalizing and standardizing workplace drug testing across Europe. The society holds annual symposiums for medical doctors and nurses whose work is in drug prevention or testing at European workplaces. A safe bet is that increasing numbers of workplaces across Europe will implement some version of drug testing.

The social and political changes described in this chapter have resulted in the growth of an industry—the drug-testing industry, which is composed of various companies and interest groups with a financial stake in the continuing war on drugs and drug testing—a central component in the nation's anti-drug-use strategies. The industry itself is a diverse one and is described in chapter 2. As is shown in chapter 3, the rise of drug-testing policies and the growth of the testing industry played crucial roles in the emergence of a newer, more fragmented industry—the detox industry—which is described with the use of corporate documents and interview data. Also described are consumers of detox products and their socially constructed meanings of drug use, their subterfuge, and the politics of their resisting public and private intrusions into their lives. Chapters 4 and 5 apply theoretical explanations to expanding social monitoring and control, as well as resistance to it.

2

The Drug-Testing Industry

Drug-Testing Pervasiveness

Before drug testing swept through the American workplace, it was first applied to disparate classes of individuals for group-specific reasons. For example, during the 1960s, drug testing became a component of successful methadone treatment programs; within the same decade, the International Olympic Committee began screening athletes for the presence of performance-enhancing drugs; during the late 1960s, before being allowed to return home from Vietnam, U.S. soldiers were tested for heroin use; and by the late 1970s, jail inmates were being systematically screened as a means of controlling drug use and drug-related criminal activities (see, e.g., Massing 1998).[1] Drug testing, on an immense scale, was first imposed on those who, at least theoretically, already had relinquished some of their personal liberties—members of the armed forces and jail and prison inmates. Once the military began testing its personnel, it did so in a big way, conducting over a million urine screenings each year since 1981. Military test results indicate significant decreases in positive findings—from 4.67 percent in 1981 to .69 percent in recent years (Ackerman 1991; Zeese 1997: 1.18).

Beyond the military, individuals under the watchful eye of the ever-expanding crime-industrial complex (viz., prisoners, probationers, and parolees) increasingly have been subject to random drug testing as a condition of their confinement or probation and parole status. Justice Department data indicate that 71 percent of jails have established drug-testing policies and procedures (Wilson 2000). Positive results often have grave consequences. For example, one's probation and parole status can be revoked, resulting in confinement in jail or prison or qualitative changes in incarceration, such as solitary confinement. Nationally, about 49 percent of adult probationers are subject to routine drug screening. As

21

is typical for this war, only 17 percent of adult probationers receive any drug treatment services ("Characteristics of adults on probation" 1997: 9; "Substance abuse and treatment of adults on probation" 1998).

The drug-testing industry, with obvious financial interests at stake, advanced its financial growth by working to expand drug testing to individuals occupying diverse settings who beforehand were exempt from such intrusions. The drug-testing industry grew nearly exponentially because of its aggressive marketing strategies and the simultaneous public campaigns of politicians, office seekers, and moral entrepreneurs. Indeed, only one month after the Supreme Court's ruling in the Tecumseh, Oklahoma, case, which allowed for drug testing students engaged in extracurricular activities, the Drug and Alcohol Testing Industry Association (DATIA), an industry trade association, hosted a comprehensive training workshop in Washington, D.C. The one-day workshop was held to educate school administrators on alcohol and drug abuse and the numerous industry drug-testing products. DATIA reportedly has eleven hundred members and claims that it has trained and certified thousands of industry professionals, including specimen collectors, third-party administrators, and in-house program managers ("Implementing a student drug and alcohol testing program" 2002).

Without governmental mandates and initiatives, it is a safe assumption that drug testing would not have reached current levels. But, with industry lobbying and the federal government's coercion of particular industries, states passed their own legislation to create drug-free workplaces and to afford employers with opportunities to maximize productivity levels, enhance their competitive locations in the marketplace, and attain their projected degrees of success. As part of government's coercive measures, most states now offer financial incentives to employers who participate in workplace drug testing. For example, some states allow employers credits on their workers' insurance policies. Other states have official public policies in support of employers. In those cases, states now proclaim that employers' discharging or disciplining employees who are in violation of drug-free workplace programs will be defined as reasonable and "for cause." Furthermore, states have shifted the legal burden of proof from employers to employees who are injured on the job and whose postaccident drug screening indicates positive results (or who refuse to be tested).[2] Thus, employers are given financial motivation directly from their states of residence for implementing drug-free workplace programs. Indeed, an American Management Association survey indicates that of companies subjecting employees to drug testing, 53 percent reportedly do so because of government mandates and incentives.

According to data on companies that test employees, drug testing increased from 21.5 percent of companies testing employees in 1987 to 84.8 percent of companies testing employees in 1993—a 250 percent increase. Recent evidence suggests that drug testing has now leveled off and in fact has decreased slightly but primarily among small businesses (Zeese 1997: 1.13). Indeed, national data indicate that 66 percent of the country's largest firms engage in some type of drug testing, a decline of 4 percent since 1999 and 8 percent since 1998 (American Management Association 2001).

Among Fortune 500 companies, during the late 1980s and early 1990s, drug testing likewise increased in use. For example, in 1985 about 18 percent of Fortune 500 companies tested their employees. The number increased to a high point of 40 percent by 1991. Among Fortune 1000 firms, 48 percent of employees are subject to drug testing (Hartwell et al. 1996).

Recent data also indicate that the larger the company, the more likely it is to impose drug testing on applicants and employees. About 71 percent of work sites with more than one thousand employees conduct drug tests and about 42 percent screen for alcohol while 40 percent of work sites with fifty to ninety-nine employees screen for drugs and 16.5 percent test for alcohol (Hartwell et al. 1996: 37). Among companies with fewer than fifty employees, only 2 percent require drug testing. Ironically, the rate of current drug use is higher among workers employed with these smaller businesses than among those working for larger ones.[3] Data indicate that 56.6 percent of current illicit drug users work at places of employment with fewer than twenty-five employees; 30.2 percent of users work for employers with between twenty-five and five hundred employees; and 13.2 percent of users are employed with organizations that have five hundred or more employees. Interestingly, rates of alcohol abuse do not vary by number of employees (*An Analysis of Worker Drug Use and Workplace Policies and Programs* 1997). Companies with unionized employees are more likely to test than nonunion firms. About 62 percent of all workers in the private sector are employed by companies that engage in drug testing and 33 percent are employed by firms that test for alcohol.

The American Management Association (AMA) began collecting data on the extent of corporate drug-testing programs in 1987. At that time, their data indicated that about 21 percent of corporations used some drug testing. By 1996, 81 percent of corporations were using one method or another to test applicants and employees ("Drug abuse and workplace demographics" 2001). During the year 2001, 67 percent of firms surveyed by the AMA required new hires or employees to submit to drug testing, a figure that declined from the high of 81 percent in 1996 (American Management Association 2001). Today tens of millions of Americans are subject to corporate drug tests (*Drug Testing: A Bad Investment* 1999).

Drug-testing prevalence varies widely across industry type. Blue-collar workers are much more likely to be subject to drug testing than white-collar employees. National data show, for example, that 60.2 percent of manufacturing sites, 53.7 percent of the wholesale and retail trade, 72.4 percent of communications, utilities, and transportation, and 69.6 percent of mining and construction industries test employees. These industries have the highest prevalence of employee drug testing. Among the least tested industries are finance, real estate, and insurance, with only 22.6 percent of companies testing; only 27.9 percent of companies within the service industry conduct tests (Hartwell et al. 1996: 38). Data on alcohol parallel those for drug testing. Workers most likely to be subjected to drug and alcohol screening are non-college-educated males who are full-time employees and union members (Hartwell, Steele, and Rodman 1998: 30). Drug testing varies by geographic region as well, with the southern United States reportedly conducting more drug testing than any other area in the country (Hartwell et al. 1996).

The body of evidence clearly shows that social class and income are inversely related to drug testing; working-class members with the lowest incomes are those most likely to be subjected to drug testing (Zeese 1997:

TABLE 2.1
Types of Testing by Percentage of Firms and Year

Type of Testing	1992	1993	1994	1995	1996	1997	1998	1999	2000	2001
Illegal or Controlled Substances	73	78	76	78	81	74	74	70	66	67
HIV Antibodies	9.5	4.4	2.5	0.7	1.2	5.2	3.9	2.8	2.6	2.2
Fitness for Duty	NA	NA	NA	NA	NA	57	58	55	48	50
STDs	NA	NA	NA	NA	NA	4	5	3	3	2

Source: American Management Association, New York, 2001.

1.16). In a private interview with the author in September 2000, one particular company's human resource manager responsible for implementing drug-testing policies describes the credentials required among his low-paid workers:

> The skill levels here will be anywhere from minimal skills required, not even sometimes a high school education, to positions in the hourly ranks that might go up into requiring a high school education and maybe even technical school.

Although managers and executives allege that testing programs are effective mechanisms for improving productivity and workplace health and safety, there is little empirical support for their claims. The most recent research indicates that drug-testing programs do not improve productivity and that companies adopting testing programs have lower levels of productivity than those that forego them (Shepard and Clifton 1998). On the other hand, recent data indicate that workplace drug-testing programs reduce injuries and workers' compensation claims. Indeed, companies using random combined with preemployment testing initiatives reduced their mean workers' compensation claims 63.7 percent over a four-year period. Companies that did not conduct drug testing witnessed their workers' compensations claims increase 19 percent during the same period ("Drug abuse and workplace demographics" 2001). (Assumptions of causality, however, are ill advised.)

The main impetus for drug-testing programs initially (and still to some extent) seemingly were politics, rhetoric, and government mandates and rewards (Normand, Lempert, and O'Brien 1994b). Today, however, given the pervasiveness of drug testing, corporate executives resign themselves to the position that screening is simply a normal and functional contemporary business practice. Since most companies use screening methods, corporate executives report that they feel obliged to follow suit, fearing that workers desiring to avoid drug testing at particular companies probably would gravitate to nontesting firms. The data support this conjecture. Current drug users indicate that they are far less likely to apply for a job when they know that the prospective employer requires preemployment or random drug testing than when testing is not a job requirement ("Drug abuse and workplace demographics" 2001). Indeed, among workers who currently use illegal drugs, 29.8 percent reported that they are less likely to work for employers requiring drug testing at hiring than for those that do not test. Among non-drug-using workers, 5.9 percent state they would not work for employers who use drug screening (*An Analysis of Worker Drug Use and Workplace Policies and Programs* 1997). Consider the following comments of one transnational corporate spokesperson:

> I think one issue that a company has to consider is that it has become pretty much a standard business practice and particularly in manufacturing to do preemployment testing. If you don't do that, then you have a chance of getting all the other rejects. Everybody that has tested positive will come here and say, "Hey, they don't test us over there." And that may just be a mental impression of what would happen. The other thing is that we take a very aggressive approach in safety. It's a pretty proven fact that people that are under the influence of either illegal drugs or even abusing prescription drugs and/or alcohol, it impairs their decision process and their mental process of making logical decisions. Sometimes, particularly in an industrial setting, you have to react rather quickly to a situation that's happened. If you're mentally impaired or not ready to make that decision, it could put you in a very hazardous situation. And I think the second thing, as part of that, is drug use in our society has gotten to be so big of a problem that employers are having to do it to protect themselves. It becomes a safety issue. Unfortunately you have to do this to protect yourself because it's become very rampant in the society that we live [in]. (Private Interview, October 2000)[4]

This representative gave three commonly volunteered explanations for drug testing among private employers: it currently is normal business practice; it serves as a mechanism for protecting employees' safety; and as a useful process for making the workplace safer, it is a safeguard for employers fearing accident-related law suits, worker-compensation claims, and the resulting and innumerable symbolic costs (e.g., public's loss of confidence, declining value of stock, investors' doubts of company leadership, etc.).

A reasonable assumption, and especially from this spokesman's rhetoric on the pervasiveness of drug use and the need to contain it, is that these initiatives as well as the broader war on drugs are political responses to public demand or concern. However, national data show that the general public mostly has defined drug abuse as a rather insignificant to moderate problem. For example, in January 1985, only 2 percent of

Americans defined drug abuse as the nation's most important problem. The numbers rose each year, to a high of 27 percent in 1989, but declined as markedly as they had increased—to 6 percent in 1993 with an increase to 17 percent in 1997, then back down to 7 percent in 2001 (Rasmussen and Benson 1994: 125; "Attitudes" 1996; *Sourcebook* 2000: 100).

Perhaps more telling, Harris Poll data indicate far lower levels of public concern about drug use. When respondents were asked for the two most important issues for the government to address, drugs consistently ranked twelfth on the list of concerns. For example, in 1993, only 3 percent of respondents reported drugs as one of the problems. In 1997, 8 percent reported drugs but the number dropped to 4 percent in 2000 (*Sourcebook* 2000: 101). All the while the American public defined a host of other social problems (especially economic concerns) as being equally as pressing as drug abuse, federal and state law makers were passing drug-war legislation, including that mandating or rewarding workplace drug testing.

The Clinton administration deviated little from its predecessors. Its efforts at ratcheting up testing included pressuring Congress to pass legislation requiring every person applying for a driver's license to submit to drug tests. Congress refused to pass such legislation (even though the American public supports it ["Attitudes" 1996]). Indeed, 76.5 percent of college freshmen favor workplace drug testing (although 52 percent favor the medicalization rather than criminalization of drug use) (*Sourcebook* 2000: 132, 179).

Legislators, however, have endorsed, to varying degrees, testing citizens who receive anything of value from federal, state, city, or county governments (e.g., welfare and food stamp benefits, public housing, general relief, free medical assistance, etc.). Likewise, testing is entering arenas once considered off limits. For example, in 1995 the Dayton County, Ohio, school district implemented a program to conduct random drug testing on student athletes. In September 1999, the 6th U.S. Circuit Court of Appeals affirmed the legality of a Knox County, Tennessee, program designed to test teachers, principals, and other school employees. Infamous Harlan County, Kentucky, during the 1999–2000 school year, initiated a random drug-testing program for all teachers, principals, and administrators (Williams 1999). And although various school districts across the country are now testing employees and student athletes, a private high school in Memphis, Tennessee, has initiated random drug testing on its entire student body, a program endorsed and financially supported (to the tune of sixty dollars per test) by parents. Students refusing to submit to testing will be expelled from school ("Private high school in Memphis" 2000). Each of these events (and others) indicates the extensiveness of drug testing within the United States. Students, to date, however, are not subject to drug testing at levels experienced by employees and job applicants.

In the next section, detailed attention is given to drug testing as a condition of employment and to current testing procedures.

Types of Drug Testing

Employers currently rely on a number of procedures for testing both employees and those seeking work. Preemployment testing (i.e., testing of job applicants) is considered a preventive strategy for employers since it denies employment to applicants identified as drug users. Nearly all companies using some mode of drug screening also use preemployment testing. It is the most broadly used type of testing; 78 percent of companies reportedly require applicants to comply with these procedures (Fay 1991: 9; cf. Hartwell et al. 1996; "Drug abuse and workplace demographics" 2001). Its widespread use probably is due, in part, to the legal advantages afforded employers; this type of drug testing contains no labor grievances or litigation since employers have no legal or contractual obligation to nonemployee applicants. Recent data show that of preemployment test results, 3.7 percent were positive (*Drug Testing Index* 1999).

Second, random or unannounced testing typically is used in occupations where public health, safety, and well-being are considered at risk (e.g., law enforcement, aviation, transportation), although construction, industry, and retail firms use this form as well. Random testing is designed to ferret out current drug-using employees who, as data indicate, are less stable with employment than non-drug-using employees. For example, among employees who currently use drugs, 32.1 percent claim to have changed jobs three or more times within the period of a year, as opposed to 17.9 percent of non-drug-using employees. Among drug users, 12.1 percent (versus 6.1 percent of nonusers) had taken an unexcused absence from work, and 4.6 percent (versus 1.4 percent of nonusers) had been terminated by an employer during the previous year (*An Analysis of Worker Drug Use and Workplace Policies and Programs* 1997). Although these are significant differences, data also show that there are vast distinctions between casual and chronic drug users. For example, there are no differences between casual drug users and nonusers in their ability to find and maintain employment (French, Roebuck, and Alexandre 2001).

Random testing has become the most common and fastest-growing drug-testing procedure for current employees, with 46.7 percent of work sites reportedly using this method (Blum et al. 1992; "Drug abuse and workplace demographics" 2001). It also remains the most controversial. Subjected to what employees define as an invasive procedure without probable cause, they report that random testing reduces them to little more than suspects. Although employers recognize that random testing is contrary to employees' wishes, they nonetheless consider it a necessary strategy and a policy that corresponds to society's interests. As a company policy, it also is supported by federal and state governments. Random test results produce positive findings of 2.5 percent (*Drug Testing Index* 1999).

The third type, reasonable cause testing, is used when an employee's job performance suggests possible drug use. Since legal stakes are higher when they engage in this type of testing, employers exercise caution in its implementation and in training supervisory personnel on testing procedures and legal obligations to employees. Even with the recognized potential for litigation, this is the second most common drug-testing procedure used on employees, with 37 percent of work sites reportedly employing this method (see, e.g., Hartwell et al. 1996). It also, not surprisingly, produces the highest positive findings—14 percent (*Drug Testing Index* 1999).

Postaccident testing, a fourth type, is used in cases where employees have been involved in on-the-job accidents. Although employees may display no signs of inebriation or of being under the influence of alcohol or drugs (e.g., slurred speech, red and glassy eyes), employers, as standard operating procedure, nonetheless test employees after on-the-job accidents. Research indicates that 26 percent of work sites use this form of testing and 3.5 percent of tests in postaccident situations are positive (Hartwell et al. 1996; *Drug Testing Index* 1999).

The fifth method, periodic testing, is used on a regular schedule, usually in conjunction with physical exams, which are required of some employees within specific occupations (e.g., law enforcement, corrections). Since employees must be given advance notice of when such physical examinations are scheduled, few employees (1.4 percent) test positive for drugs. Only 13.7 percent of work sites claim to use this testing method (*Drug Testing Index* 1999).

The sixth procedure, rehabilitation testing, is used with those employees who have tested positive earlier and, as a condition of continued employment, are engaged in counseling, rehabilitation, and periodic drug testing as a form of monitoring their sobriety and abstinence. Of those tested, 4.6 percent produce positive results (Fay 1991; *Drug Testing Index* 1999).

Most current drug-testing programs are designed to test all employees (e.g., through random testing) and job applicants (e.g., through preemployment screening (Hartwell et al. 1996). It is the preemployment variety to which most working men and women are subject and to which the next section is devoted.

Preemployment Testing

Preemployment screening currently is the most commonly used type of drug testing. Seventy-eight percent of companies require job-applicant drug testing, although, as stated earlier, it is more common among larger than smaller firms and among blue-collar than white-collar occupations. Larger companies employ staff (e.g., company nurses) to secure samples from applicants. Samples are analyzed on the premises. In cases where a positive result is determined, the sample usually is sent to an accredited laboratory for corroborating testing. Other companies send job applicants to doctors' offices or clinics for the testing and interpreting of results. Medical doctors in these cases are referred to as medical review officers—a title that conveys a degree of power and authority (as in law enforcement, parole, and truant officer) and one that symbolically communicates an active participation in a quasi-militarized antidrug campaign that relies heavily on surveillance.[5] Other companies contract with laboratories and send urine samples directly to them by courier. Still others ship urine samples to various regions of the country where centralized laboratories under contract perform the urinalyses.

Testing typically is not a part of the application process per se. Rather, it begins once applicants are made clear that a job offer will be made but that it is conditional on their passing a drug test. Although justification of this procedure may involve hair-splitting semantics, companies evidently are on less shaky legal ground when explaining preemployment testing in these terms. Consider the rhetoric used by one industrial company's representative when explaining its preemployment processes. As can be gleaned from the following, the company conducts its own on-site tests and simple analyses.

A: At this location, at the current time, the only drug testing we do is preemployment. Actually, it's more of a postemployment because you can't do preemployment testing any more. We take applications here at the facility. Usually the same day that they fill it out, we try to spend ten to fifteen minutes with the person and interview that person in what I would call a mini-interview. And at that time we sort of classify that person into the type of positions that they fill into the production plant. Then, as we get openings, we go back to that pool of people and say, "OK, we have this opening that requires XYZ, oh, and here we have an applicant that has XYZ. There's a match. Let's call them in." We get with the applicant and have them come in for a guided tour of the facility. As part of the tour of the facility they are asked to have a drug screen on-site.

Q: Unannounced?

A: Unannounced. And that is performed and we have immediate results. It's a positive or a negative. It's a pass or fail. If we have a negative, that's fine and we can go to the next step in the hiring process. If we have a positive, which means they have failed the drug test for some reason, then they are given an appointment with the company physician and that physician does a second drug test using an accredited lab. The first test is not using an accredited lab. To take the initial sample to a lab is fairly expensive. But, the test kit, I've forgotten the numbers, is fairly reliable.

(Private Interview, October 1999)

In addition to the information offered by this human resource officer on preemployment testing processes, he also spoke of testing-related costs and the realization that their procedures are only "fairly reliable." Throughout the data-collection processes for this research, corporate spokespersons, as a group, almost always defined testing costs as reasonable and worthwhile expenditures. While recognizing that accuracy may be a problem, they nonetheless remain confident in the marvels of modern testing technologies and in their abilities to delineate the reputable from the disreputable by a single measure of positive or negative. (It's a "yes or no," said one corporate representative, describing what is learned from drug testing.)

Among companies that require preemployment screening, less than 1 percent hire and 30 percent permanently disqualify applicants testing positive. Procedures in other companies allow applicants to reapply six months after having failed a drug-screening test. An indication of the widespread use of preemployment testing is the fact that temporary employment agencies are increasingly requiring this type of drug screening. According to these agencies, potential employers are demanding that transient workers also verify that they are drug-free.

Employers consider preemployment testing as the screening method that presents the fewest number of personnel and legal challenges. Since employers can hire whomever they wish (if they are compliant with civil rights laws), applicants have no expectation of employment and no property right to a given job to which they have only applied. Since no contract has been offered, there are no damages incurred when employment is denied.

Preemployment testing theoretically determines which applicants are drug free. This initial test generally satisfies employers and their policies for maintaining a drug-free workplace. During this research, employers, as a group, acknowledged that preemployment testing is a relatively easy and inexpensive method for ensuring a drug-free work force. One corporate manager described the costs of in-house screening versus screening using an external and accredited laboratory.

A: Generally speaking, if we would go to the physician to do the drug testing, it would run anywhere between thirty and fifty dollars, sometimes even more than that in a hospital setting. If we have an emergency setting, it would cost even more. The test kit is around fourteen to fifteen dollars. So, it's about half the cost. But, there's a trade-off here though. If we use the normal lab process they basically look at ten different drugs. The test kit only looks at five.

Q: Do you know which five?

A: Basically the illegal five, the illegal drugs. What this means is marijuana, cocaine, those types of drugs. The hard drugs.

(Private Interview, November 1999)

This employer, like most interviewed, reflected current political rhetoric about drugs by defining marijuana as a "hard" drug and also determined that the costs of using in-house methods are acceptable, indeed preferable, to the costs of using external processes. Recent research has led to some recommendations that workplace policies on insurance and employee-assistance programs recognize that there are clear distinctions between casual and chronic drug users as well as their impact on insurance, longevity, absenteeism, and overall job performance (French, Roebuck, and Alexandre 2001).

Preemployment testing also is considered a way of reducing the likelihood of hiring drug-using employees, who have higher absentee and tardiness rates than drug-free employees. Data on those testing positive and those testing negative on issues of absenteeism, turnover, and use of sick leave do indicate differences between these groups. The same distinctions are also evident for alcohol.

Drug testing is pervasive and employers offer all kinds of explanations for using such policies even when so few individuals (and fewer each year) test positive and despite the fact that drug use among full-time workers has remained stable (viz., between 7 and 8 percent) across the past decade (*Drug Testing Index* 1999; *An Analysis of Worker Drug Use and Workplace Policies and Programs* 1997). Consider the following conversation with a company's personnel officer:

Q: Do you know what percentage of people you test show up positive?

A: I don't know if I could give you that actual number because I don't know if we track that. I will tell you that it's relatively small. They know we test, they tend to stay away from us. I think particularly the heavier users because obviously they'll have a harder time bypassing the system than a casual user. And I think casual users are the ones that are likely to get caught up in your system not recognizing that there is going to be a drug test or maybe not even thinking they're going to get caught. If you don't do drug testing and you have people that use drugs out on the floor. . . . I'm not sure I've ever seen anything that says that their longevity is going to be less than that of a nonuser. But, to say it's a dollar and cents issue, I don't think I could say that because I don't know if I personally agree with that. My two years of exposure to random testing, in that particular time we tested about twelve people per quarter. So, we were testing forty to fifty people per year. If I re-member in two years I had two positives. We're not catching very many people.

(Private Interview, September 1999)

And another personnel manager offered a similar rationale:

Q: Do you think your program is cost effective?
A: I don't have a good answer to that because I've often wondered the same thing. Because you have such a small turn-down rate that you have to say, "In dollars and cents, does it really make sense to do that?" I think it's a legitimate question for everyone to look at and is one that I have not an answer for because we do spend a fair amount of money in testing. And you say, "Are you getting the bang for your buck" type of thing? I guess this is a place where you really don't get a whole lot, but you just don't know how many are not coming to your door because they know you do it and that's the part you can't measure because you just don't know those things. You just have to make an assumption that if I didn't do it, it would be a whole lot worse than if I do do it. It's more of an assumption than an actual reality.

(Private Interview, February 2000)

His rationale is supported by *National Household Survey on Drug Abuse* data. Among workers who currently use illicit drugs, 29.8 percent claim that they would not work for an employer who uses preemployment screening whereas only 5.9 percent of non-drug-using workers make this claim (*An Analysis of Worker Drug Use and Workplace Policies and Programs* 1997).

Given the widespread use of drug testing, surprisingly few companies have engaged in any program evaluation of its effectiveness or financial costs versus benefits. This is an interesting contrast to companies' routine evaluations of the effectiveness of various strategies used in manufactur-ing and personnel matters. In fact, in 1996 the American Management Association surveyed corporations who have used and currently use drug-testing programs and asked if they had any primary evidence that their programs were cost effective. Only 8 percent reported having con-ducted any cost-benefit analyses (American Management Association 1996).

Most job applicants know whether or not a prospective employer requires preemployment drug screening. As a result, few job applicants test positive for drugs. This means, then, that the total cost of each positive discovery, including all negative results and costlier confirmatory tests, is about eighty-five hundred dollars. The federal government, during a one-year period, spent $11.7 million on testing employees (rather than applicants) in thirty-eight different agencies. About twenty-nine thousand drug tests were performed and 153 of the results (.5 percent) were positive. Thus, detecting one single positive case cost nearly seventy-seven thousand dollars (*Drug Testing: A Bad Investment* 1999). Yet employers claim that they reap intangible rewards from their testing policies and procedures. For example, they enjoy a confidence that they are keeping their workplace drug free and as a result benefiting monetarily. They also are financially rewarded for implementing testing strategies by their states and the insurance companies with whom they do business. National data suggest that over half of employers surveyed consider the benefits (no matter how defined) from drug testing as outweighing the costs. Employers define drug testing as the method of choice for countering drug use in the workplace. In fact, 40.6 percent of employers claim it is more important to use drug testing than to have an employee assistance program while only 7.8 percent believed it was more important to have an employee assistance program than to drug test ("Drug abuse and workplace demographics" 2001). Such evidence is an affirmation of employers' confidence in drug testing as the single most effective strategy for weeding out drug-using employees.

Drug testing in the workplace has often been and continues to be explained as companies' acquiescing to public demand for such programs. Corporations often tout their drug -testing policies as resulting from increasing levels of intolerance of drug use among workers, consumers, and society generally. They reason that drug testing is a way to appease their employees (and stockholders) who do not want to work or associate with users of illicit drugs. Consider the following corporate spokesperson's explanation:

> In part, we test because of pressure from the employees, employees that are nonusers of drugs. They say, "Hey, I don't want to work around people who use drugs." I think there's a fair amount of pressure; there's a fair amount of that in smoking today. Nonsmokers don't want it and they're pushing the smoker in a different direction. And I think there's a

lot of our society that is saying, "Hey, you ought to do this because it's the right thing to do, to help our society become drug free." And I think there is probably some psychological stuff underneath the covers, if you will, of doing that too for companies today. I think we have a moral obligation and obviously a business obligation, but I think sometimes a moral obligation to do the right thing with people in communities. I think that's probably the idea, the more I think about it. (Private Interview, October 2000)[6]

Preemployment testing, however, is not solely a corporate initiative. Courts have greatly contributed to the increased use of this type of screening. To date, courts have expanded the scope of the *Skinner* and *Von Raab* cases by applying them to preemployment drug testing. Challenges to court rulings have originated almost solely from the public rather than private sector. The United States Court of Appeals for the First Circuit, regarding preemployment drug testing, ruled that unions do not have standing to bring suit since applicants are not employees and since union members themselves, the majority of whom are employed, are not likely to face preemployment tests. Perhaps affected by the aforementioned court cases, the National Labor Relations Board ruled that since applicants are not employees they are unprotected by union contracts and unions' official positions on drug testing. Hence, applicants are unprotected by the Fourth and Fifth Amendments, statutory law, common law, union contracts, and labor board rulings. Applicant testing is a highly coercive procedure imposed on, in may cases, desperate and unemployed individuals. As a result, neither reasonable suspicion nor courts' efforts at balancing individual rights to privacy with the "special needs" logic applies to applicants since they, by their very acquiescence, comply with testing as a criterion for employment.

States have passed their own legislation regulating preemployment testing that mostly conforms to the logic of the *Skinner* and *Von Raab* decisions. For example, states typically allow testing if applicants are informed of the test at the time of application, if they are given a copy of the test results, and if testing complies with procedural safeguards (e.g., handling and noncontamination proceedings). In general, employers have the legal right to drug test job applicants as long as (1) the applicant knows that drug testing is part of the screening process for all new employees; (2) the applicant has already been offered the job; (3) each applicant is tested similarly; and (4) tests are conducted by state-certified

State-sanctioned notice of corporate drug testing.

YOUR
COMPANY
LETTERHEAD

I hereby consent to submit to urinalysis and/or other tests as shall be determined by [Company Name] in the selection process of applicants for employment, for the purpose of determining the drug content thereof.

I agree that

_____

(name of physician or clinic)

may collect these specimens for these tests and may test them or forward them to a testing laboratory designated by the company for analysis.

I further agree to and hereby authorize the release of the results of said tests to the company.

I understand that it is the current illegal use of drugs and/or abuse of alcohol that prohibits me from being employed at this Company.

I further agree to hold harmless the Company and its agents (including the above named physician or clinic) from any liability arising in whole or part out of the collection of specimens, testing, and use of the information from said testing in connection with the Company's consideration of my employment application.

I further agree that a reproduced copy of this pre-employment consent and release form shall have the same force and effect as the original.

I have carefully read the foregoing and fully understand its contents. I acknowledge that my signing of this consent and release form is a voluntary act on my part and that I have not been coerced into signing this document by anyone.

Applicant:
Print Name _____ S.S.#: _____ - ___ - _____

Applicant:
Signature _____ Date: ____ / ____ / _____

Witness Printed Name: _____

Witness Signature: _____

Drug-testing consent form required of applicants.

laboratories or state-approved testing measures. If applicants refuse to comply, the job offer can be legally withdrawn and employers protected by state law. Generally, applicants remain unprotected by statute.

Longitudinal data indicate steady increases in applicant testing through the economic expansion of the mid- to late 1990s. According to the American Management Association, workplace testing declined during the last half of the 1990s due to increasing costs and tighter labor markets (Nakashima 2001). With tighter labor markets, low unemployment rates, and employers competing in new ways for workers, speculative observations are that some companies may discontinue drug testing job applicants (Whitaker 1999). Speculations abound over just how employers will respond given the realities of a dynamic labor market.

Drug-Screening Methods and Procedures

Testing methods and specimen media are varied. Among those companies subjecting applicants and employees to drug tests, 82.1 percent use urine; 12.9 percent use blood; 1.1 percent use hair; and .9 percent use performance testing. Urine clearly is the medium of choice. Most drug metabolites can be detected in urine for up to three days after the drug was used; others are detectable for as long as three to four weeks after last use (e.g., marijuana used by heavy or chronic smokers) (Timrots 1992; Syva Company 1992).

Two primary methods of detecting drugs in urine dominate the testing industry—immunoassays and chromatography. Several different varieties of the immunoassays are available and are used in testing procedures. For example, the Enzyme-Multiplied Immunoassay Technique (EMIT), the Enzyme-Linked Immunosorbent Assay (the ELISA test) and Radioimmunoassay (the RIA test) are among the most commonly used. With these methods, a given urine sample is compared to a calibrator that contains a known quantity of the drug for which tests are being conducted. If the sample is equal to or higher than the calibrator, the test result is positive; if not, it is interpreted as negative (Timrots 1992). The immunoassays are considered screening tests and although reliability at one time was a significant problem, improvements have resulted in current accuracy levels of 95 to 99 percent. Nonetheless, as is discussed later, even such remarkable precision leaves room for thousands of inaccurate results and far costlier confirmatory testing.

Regarding chromatography procedures, the Gas Chromatography/ Mass Spectrometry (GC/MS) technique is the most accurate for detecting drugs in body fluids. To date, courts accept screening tests as 100 percent accurate as long as they are followed by a GC/MS confirmation. The confirmatory test costs considerably more than the initial screening—forty to seventy-five dollars—and the testing equipment itself is high tech and expensive (Tulacz and O'Toole 1991: 9). The GC/MS machine manufactured by Hewlett Packard costs about seventy-five thousand dollars, according to a testing laboratory's president (Private Interview, February 1999). About 70 percent of employers, when faced with a positive urine sample, require more rigorous, confirmatory testing (such as the GC/MS). However, 13 percent use the same procedure (such as EMIT) a second time on the same sample, 5 percent test a new sample, and 7 percent perform no confirmatory test (and simply disqualify applicants or respond in various ways to positive-testing employees). Of those companies that rely on urinalysis for detecting drug metabolites, 79 percent use National Institute on Drug Abuse–certified laboratories. Among other companies relying on urinalysis, 48 percent use medical review officers to analyze findings, compare them to individuals' medical condition and history, and submit a verdict about the test result. Today, there are over a dozen initial screening tests accepted by the scientific community although three tests dominate private and military applications—EMIT, RIA, and Thin Layered Chromatography (TLC).

EMIT and RIA use immunoassays that are synthetically produced. In the process, a controlled substance (e.g., the drug that tests are designed to detect) is bound to a naturally occurring compound (typically a protein). The result is a conjugate that is then injected into a live, nonhuman animal. Within about three weeks, the animal's immune system (more specifically, the liver), produces antibodies that negate the effects of the foreign substance. EMIT, which is manufactured by Syva in Palo Alto, California, relies on sheep for the production of the THC (the active ingredient in marijuana) assay while Roche Diagnostics uses antibodies from rabbits, goats, and donkeys for its LSD and PCP assays (Hoffman and Silvers 1987: chapter 12). The antibodies are removed through blood withdrawn from the nonhuman animals and then processed into antiserum that then seeks out the targeted drug when mixed with a subject's urine.[7]

The immunoassay EMIT was first made available by Syva in 1972. Each immunoassay uses antibodies that react with a specific drug for which the urine or blood sample is being tested. In the test mixture, the antibodies attach to the drug (if present in the sample). Several dozen assays currently are available with the ability to detect both legal and illegal substances—from marijuana to lithium. The chemical composition of a particular drug is broken down in the body, which then forms a number of compounds, or metabolites. Over one hundred different drug metabolites can be detected by immunoassays. To determine the presence of a drug, EMIT measures changes in the amount of light absorbed by the urine sample, which is an indication of the amount of drug metabolite contained in the sample and which is compared to a calibrator containing a fixed amount of the drug. The greater the amount of drug in a sample, the greater the response produced. Syva's EMIT requires little professional training and is highly sensitive to small traces of drug metabolites.

Some drugs are absorbed into the blood stream rather quickly (such as smoked marijuana or cocaine), while other delivery systems slow the rate of absorption (such as ingested marijuana or snorted cocaine). Cocaine has a half-life of one hour and is metabolized through the liver, producing minor metabolites. As a result, cocaine appears in the urine only briefly, first at about four hours after use, and is detectable for at most two to four days. Marijuana, on the other hand, is nearly completely metabolized by the body through oxidation. It is excreted in the urine within a few hours of ingestion but detection varies greatly across user type; occasional use can be detected up to one day while chronic use may be detected for three to four weeks afterwards. Given that marijuana is the most frequently used and widely distributed illegal drug in the United States and that it is detectable for such a long period after use, it is hardly surprising that marijuana is the illegal drug most commonly detected through urinalyses. More than 40 percent of individuals testing positive indicate marijuana use.

Radioimmunoassay (RIA) has been manufactured since 1972 by Roche Diagnostics, a division of the pharmaceutical giant Hoffmann-LaRoche, and has been sold commercially as Abuscreen. Rather than connecting a drug to an enzyme chain (as EMIT does), Abuscreen uses radioactive iodine as a bonding agent. The degree of bonding indicates the presence of a targeted drug (such as marijuana). This method is inexpensive, quick, simple, and automated for large numbers of samples. As a result, the Department of Defense has used this method for testing all of its enlisted personnel. Although widely used, RIA has been found to have greater levels of cross-reactivity than EMIT. Both have their positive and negative features. For example, RIA provides a quantitative measure of a drug's presence while EMIT screens for a larger number of drugs. Both tests recommend a followup procedure (such as GC/MS) for a definitive determination. Because RIA uses radioactive substances, laboratories must be certified by the Nuclear Regulatory Commission.

Thin-Layered Chromatography (TLC), which has existed for forty or more years, was used nearly exclusively in hospital settings until the recent and explosive war on drugs. Now it serves as a testing procedure for screening employees and applicants. TLC is marketed as an alternative to EMIT, but its use in drug screening is nowhere near as widespread, in part because it is not automated and, as a result, is more labor intensive, time consuming, and costly. Unlike EMIT and RIA, it is unable to detect small traces of drugs. The Toxi-Lab system (a TLC method), manufactured by Marion Laboratories, has detection cut-off points that are seven times higher than those used in EMIT. TLC also is prone to cross-reactivity problems. These three screening procedures (EMIT, RIA, and TLC) account for about 75 percent of all initial drug-screening tests (Private Interview with medical review officer, March 1999; Hoffman and Silvers 1987: 203).

The most sophisticated equipment and procedure is the Gas Chromatography/Mass Spectrometry (GC/MS) manufactured by Hewlett Packard. Specimens are subject to an electron bombardment that breaks them down into basic molecules. Measures of velocity and atomic weight, among other properties, are computer generated. The GC/MS equipment is expensive and the testing procedures themselves cost more than other methods. Evidently the investment is worthwhile for the GC/MS is the most reliable testing method available and is used primarily to confirm initial positive results. Indeed, courts have ruled that terminating employees on the basis of only a single unconfirmed EMIT test is arbitrary and capricious (*Jones v. McKenzie*). The United States Supreme Court upheld testing if positive results are confirmed through the use of GC/MS procedures (*Samuel K. Skinner v. Railway Labor Executives' Association et al.*).

The testing industry contains many invested parties and players, most of whom benefit financially from workplace drug testing. As testing has become commonplace, the list of those profiting has grown to include, for example, pharmaceutical manufacturers, laboratory groups, diagnostic firms, private and public security and law enforcement agencies, health and social service providers, law firms, lobbyists, health clinics and health personnel, medical doctors serving as medical review officers (MROs),

Random access for process efficiency in the TDx tradition

Efficient operational flexibility

- *Random access* optimizes testing to meet individual work flow needs.
- *Batch* operation performs higher-volume testing quickly and economically.
- Testing available around the clock.

Proven accuracy and reliability

- FPIA technology offers accuracy, precision, sensitivity, and specificity for reliable results.
- Stable calibration saves time and money.

Easy-to-use automation

1 Load reagent carousel   2 Load sample carousel   3 Designate reagent selection   4 Press run

Abbott Diagnostics' TDx System. *Courtesy of Abbot Laboratories.*

43

consultants, and of course the crime-industrial complex (Walsh and Trumble 1991: 22). Profits associated with drug testing accelerated by 10 percent per year from the mid-1980s through the 1990s and continue unabated. Today's testing enterprise is a multi-billion-dollar industry.

A number of corporations manufacture testing equipment designed for use in laboratories and medical facilities, places of employment, homes, and schools. Some corporate manufacturers are household names; others are less well known. One of the more widely recognized companies, Abbott Laboratories, manufactures a drug-testing kit designed to stand alone and apart from medical facilities. Designed to test urine, the system is known as Rapid Drug Screen, or RDS. Abbott also manufactures the TDx system, designed to conduct therapeutic drug monitoring. The TDx is designed to test large numbers of specimens at incredible speeds. It also includes a bar code scanning device that automates the input of specimen identifiers, which reduces operators' labor and associated costs. The TDx system allows employers to conduct their own on-site analyses for the presence of cocaine, barbiturates, and PCP. The TDx system uses assays to conduct preliminary analytical tests with a recommendation for followup GC/MS testing.

Roche Diagnostics manufactures several drug-testing devices. The most commonly used at this time, the "OnTrak TesTcup-5" (or simply Testcup), is a urine-specimen cup used for the detection of drug metabolites. This device is designed to generate a blue color on the side of the cup if the test result is negative and a white color if it is positive. Five drugs (viz., amphetamine, cocaine, marijuana, morphine and PCP), which are listed on the cup's side, are detectable with this device. Roche also manufactures and markets the OnTrak "TesTstik," which is used to test for the presence of the same five specific drugs. The TesTstik is actually dipped into a urine sample; a color change to blue indicates a negative result.

Syva has been the leading developer and manufacturer of drug-testing systems for about thirty years. Its products are sold in more than forty-five countries worldwide. The company makes the commonly used EMIT assay and an on-site rapid-test kit used by employers at the workplace.

As stated earlier, Hewlett Packard manufactures the precise confirmatory testing machine—the Gas Chromatography Mass Spectrogram or GC/MS. Hewlett Packard also makes a liquid chromatography mass spectrogram (LC/MS).

The meteoric rise in employee and applicant drug testing has been a boon to various clinics, laboratories, diagnostic centers, and medical re-

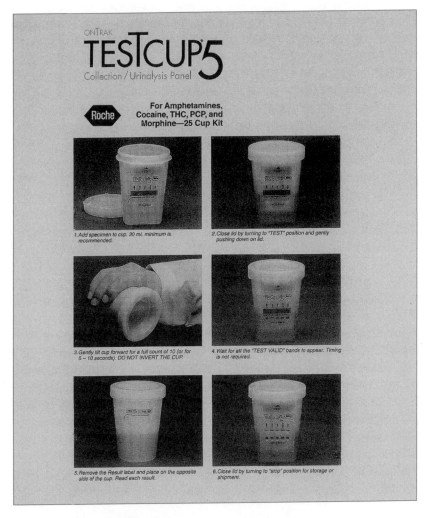

Roche Diagnostics' TesTstick.
Courtesy of F. Hoffman–La Roche Ltd.

view officers. Indeed, data indicate that outside contractors (rather than employers themselves) are responsible for drug testing at 79 percent of work sites that require testing. One of the country's largest diagnostic firms, Quest Diagnostic, analyzes about 40 percent of all tests nationwide for a total of 6.3 million tests processed in the year 2001 ("Firms offer ways to foil drug tests" 2003). Employers' medical departments conduct

Roche Diagnostics' TesTcup-5 and TesTstick. *Courtesy of F. Hoffman–La Roche Ltd. Courtesy of F. Hoffman–La Roche Ltd.*

tests at about 11 percent of work sites, and 6.4 percent use screening conducted by personnel or human resources departments (Hartwell et al. 1996). The drug-testing phenomenon has clearly created another industry, that of outside contractors. One medical review officer described her business operation:

> A: We just collect samples here and, by courier, send them to Austin Hills. We're hooked to their computer and have the results in forty-eight hours. If it comes back positive, we talk to the person to see if something other than the illegal drug might have given us the positive read, such as prescription medicine.
>
> Q: Do you do many of these?
>
> A: Oh, yeah. Lots of employers now require these tests and we have contracts with a lot of different employers.
>
> (Private Interview, April 2000)

In the back of the building housing that particular medical facility is a mobile lab, a large bus used for collecting on-site urine samples, that had on its back door a posted sign reading, "Wait Quietly Please."

The only drug-testing laboratory in a major economic region of Tennessee has six major companies under contract (including Manpower) and also conducts urinalyses for four doctor's offices (including MROs). About 80 percent of their testing is on preemployment applicants, mainly manufacturing and temporary workers, another indicator of the skewed direction of testing. The laboratory conducts only urine testing and, according to the lab's president, for good reason.

> A: Urine is the best way to go; it's more reliable, you can freeze it and it will last forever. Urine stands up in court whereas hair and saliva have not been tested in court cases. We use EMIT as a screening test. Our machine can do one hundred samples per hour. If we get a positive, we use the GC/MS.
>
> Q: Is cross-reactivity much of an issue?
>
> A: Cross-reactivity used to be a problem, but now EMIT is quite good. As long as the procedures are sound, the testing is very reliable. For example, only about 1 percent of THC found is a false positive and about 10 percent of opiates. That's when we do a GC/MS where the chances of a false positive are infinitesimal.
>
> (Personal Interview, December 1999)

Other testing methods and procedures currently are used but nowhere near as widely as those mentioned above. For example, Keystone Medical Corporation in Columbia, Maryland, manufactures the KDI Qwik Test for screening in the home. Diagnostics Products Corporation manufactures a system for analyzing saliva; and American Drug Screening in Dallas manufactures AWARE, which is marketed for home use but requires shipping the urine sample, which is then subject to EMIT testing (see, e.g., Hoffman and Silvers 1987: chapter 12). PharmChem in California is a major urine testing company. Urine samples are shipped there and results faxed to the contractor within forty-eight hours. Phamatech of San Diego, California, manufactures the Quick Screen at Home Drug Test available to both employers and parents.

The most recent arrival on the scene, which has not yet experienced any sort of financial take-off, is a test manufactured by E.K. Tech. The system is designed to jettison the urine sample directly down the toilet bowl and dehydrate it, all while its computers perform nearly instantaneous analyses. E.K. Tech also manufactures electronic scramblers, descramblers, and radar detection devices, which are corporate manufactured and marketed devices of resistance (and are further discussed in chapter 5).

Syva manufactures a do-it-yourself drug-detection kit—the RapidTest —a hand-held testing device that provides results in three to five minutes and is marketed as "fast, accurate, and cost-effective." It is used in both public and private employment settings.

Although urine is the medium of choice for drug screening, hair follicle testing, which is much more precise at detecting the presence of drugs, is becoming more widely used. A safe assumption is that as the cost of hair testing decreases and as courts rule on its validity and reliability, it will probably become the preferred mode for private and public agencies. Hair testing requires about an inch of hair, which usually is taken from the subject's head. However, very short hair poses problems, leaving subjects and those collecting samples in the awkward position of collecting hair from elsewhere on the body.

Regarding hair analyses, although the exact causes remain a mystery, dark-haired people and African Americans are more likely to test positive than blondes or Caucasians. Speculation is that drugs are more readily absorbed into dark hair. Some hair treatments have been known to affect detection reliability. Urine testing generally will reveal drugs consumed within the past two or three days. Blood testing generally will disclose

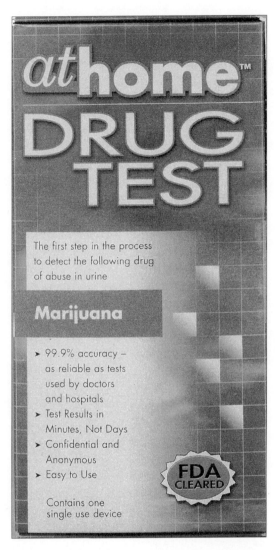

Phamatech Quick Screen at Home Drug Test for surveilling family members' or one's own marijuana use. *Courtesy of Phamatech.*

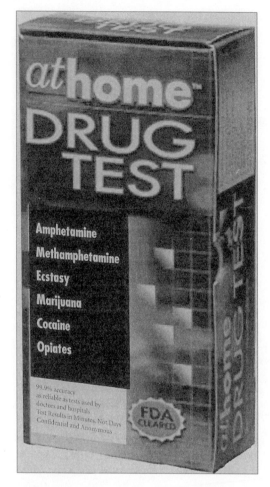

Phamatech Quick Screen at Home Drug Test
for detecting a variety of drugs. *Courtesy of
Phamatech.*

drugs used within the past two to twenty-two hours. Hair testing, by
comparison, exposes drug use during the previous week to two months,
which raises further criticism of this method's detection of previous rather
than current drug use.

The Food and Drug Administration (FDA) has long treated the numerous home drug-test kits as highly politicized since the kits enable in-

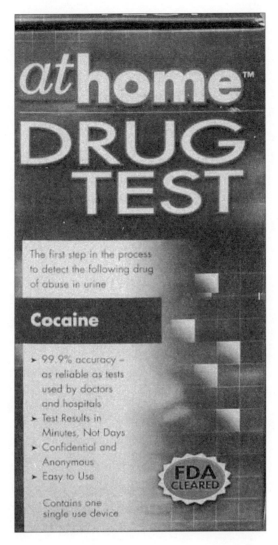

Phamatech Quick Screen at Home Drug Test for
surveilling family members' or one's own cocaine
use. *Courtesy of Phamatech.*

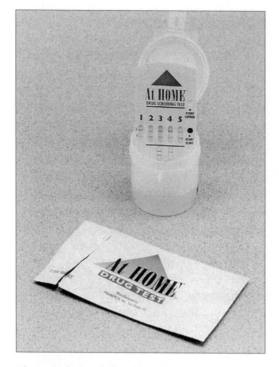

Phamatech Quick Screen at Home Drug Test for
surveilling family members or checking oneself.
Courtesy of Phamatech.

trafamily surveillance. But, in February 1997, the FDA adopted a policy
removing the requirement of premarket approval for companies selling
nonprescription drug-test kits. The agency's adopted policy requires that
three criteria for premarket approval be met: (1) home drug-test kit companies must use only FDA-approved tests, (2) testing methods must conform to specific labeling methods and procedures, and (3) testing results
must be generated by certified laboratories. Given the FDA's action, the
market will probably expand with the arrival of newer and less expensive
testing kits.

The FDA also recently approved the manufacture of saliva-testing procedures. Epitope has begun developing testing processes using the RIA to
detect the presence of drugs in saliva. Marketed by OraSure Technolo-

gies, the oral fluid testing is designed to detect illicit drugs as well as alcohol. OraSure's device, Intercept, allegedly simplifies collection, minimizes adulteration of the sample, and produces faster and less expensive results than other methods. It is marketed for the workplace as well as for criminal-justice agencies, drug-rehabilitation clinics, and hospital emergency and psychiatric wards. A newer technique is the Sweat Patch. Recently FDA approved, the patch is most commonly used by individuals on probation and parole. It is hailed as tamper proof and each patch has its own serial number. In due time, and with increasingly sophisticated techniques, urine may no longer be the preferred medium for drug testing.

Drug-Testing Inadequacies

Employers and laboratory officials agree on the broad range of substances for testing, the threshold levels of drug metabolites that meet their definition of a positive result, and the option of retesting positive cases using similar or other procedures. Nearly all companies testing employees for alcohol also test for illegal (and some legal) drugs. Few companies testing for illegal drugs also test for alcohol (Hartwell et al. 1996). The irony is obvious. Data consistently show that it is alcohol rather than drug abuse that is most frequently associated with those work-related problems that drug-testing measures theoretically are aimed at minimizing (e.g., absenteeism, job turnover, accidents, poor performance, theft, vandalism, and negative work behaviors). Alcohol abuse in the workplace continues to be addressed through less formal and punitive procedures than drug use. Although evidence suggests that alcohol testing is on the rise, individuals defined as abusing alcohol, unlike those abusing drugs, were until recently protected by the Americans with Disabilities Act and employees were considered a "medically protected group." In most cases, alcohol-related job-performance impairment must be confirmed before workers can be sanctioned (Hartwell, Steele, and Rodman 1998: 28, 33).

In reality, individuals manifesting alcohol problems (such as coming to work under the influence) are often responded to far less punitively than those discovered using or having used illegal drugs. Employee assistance in the form of counseling and rehabilitation has become the standard corporate response to alcohol abuse. Drug use is responded to, most often, through formal sanctions; the employee often is dismissed and the applicant denied employment and consideration for employment for a fixed period (e.g., six months to indefinitely).

Drug testing has other drawbacks. Urine testing cannot show whether the person being tested has a drug problem. Nor can it show whether the person is under the drug's influence, or impaired or intoxicated. All that a urine test can measure is the presence of metabolites of that substance. Since individual metabolic rates differ, it is virtually impossible to detect impairment level through any examination of drug metabolites in urine. Interestingly, an infrequent user who consumes a drug just prior to a test, even if impaired, more than likely will not test positive since the drug has not yet been metabolized. Yet a chronic user, who, because of an impending drug test, may discontinue drug use for several days may still test positive.

EMIT urine assays cannot measure the amount of a drug present in urine samples. They only provide a positive or negative result (established by comparison to a calibrator containing a known quantity of a drug). As a result, the degree of drug usage by the individual being tested is unknown and, indeed, unknowable.

Another significant problem with drug testing is the issue of cross-reactivity or confusing one substance for another (e.g., the proverbial poppy seed bagel for opium-based drugs). The most popular screening procedures can mistake a dozen or more other substances for illegal drug metabolites. EMIT, for example, has been known to mistake ibuprofen for marijuana. Biosite Test Kits, used by 45 percent of U.S. hospitals for screening emergency room patients (among others), often mistake the antiulcer drug Protonix for marijuana (Stambaugh 2002). Indeed, the realities of cross-reactivity are part of the reliability measures of drug-screening tests and procedures.

Accuracy, which is a significant problem for urinalysis, is dependent on a sample's ambient conditions—temperature and pH level. Urine ideally has a pH of 5.5 to 8.0 and a temperature close to 98.6° F. Urine-sample containers come equipped with a thermometer that changes color as it approaches body temperature, making it easy for nearly any tester to monitor temperature. Accuracy itself is a statistical probability that is affected by the sensitivity (i.e., the ability to detect drugs in very small concentrations) and specificity (i.e., the ability to differentiate between substances) of particular testing procedures. Sensitivity, or lack thereof, contributes to false negatives (i.e., drugs are present but undetected) while specificity contributes to cross-reactivity or false positives (i.e., drugs are not present but the test result is positive) (see, e.g., Hoffman and Silvers 1987: chapter 12). Testing accuracy is close to 95 percent. A rate of 5 percent inaccuracy may appear innocuous until one considers the sheer number of individuals tested (e.g., fifty thousand inaccurate results out of one million tests). Those false positives are typically subjected to confirmatory and costlier testing. In the meantime, the individuals involved are falsely accused or at the least suspected. As a result, increasing numbers of testing laboratories and employers subject positive samples to further confirmatory procedures (such as the GC/MS).

The Syva Company recognizes that false positives are possible outcomes of drug testing and cautions users of its EMIT assay of such potential problems. Chemical false positives also occur if the sample is contaminated by another substance or during handling and analyses—in other words, due to human error. A variety of other errors also complicate urinalyses results. For example, there may be inconsistencies in laboratory techniques; technicians make human errors. Also, discriminating between drugs becomes difficult with a time lag between sample collection and analysis (Lewis et al. 1972).

Testing inadequacies are a reality of drug-screening policies and procedures. Yet, industry and government remain confident in the marvels of modern testing methods.

Conclusion

The drug-testing industry is the quintessential example of modernity. Its profound faith in technology; its underlying philosophy of surveillance; its ability to process large numbers of samples; and its confidence in science as a means of social control—each suggests modern strategies and ideologies for addressing complex social issues. The drug-testing industry undoubtedly has generated a number of for-profit companies that hire large numbers of individuals and whose production contributes markedly to the national economy. One latent consequence of the emergence of this industry is its impact on the rise of the testing industry's antithesis—a fragmented detox industry composed of several companies manufacturing products designed to generate false-negative test results. It is this detox industry that receives attention in the next chapter.

3

The Detox Industry

The detox industry is composed of a consortium of companies each offering numerous yet similar commodities. No matter the product, each is designed, at least theoretically, to produce a false-negative drug-test result (i.e., nondetection of drugs despite their presence). As detailed in this chapter, within the industry there essentially are two types of detox company: one that markets its products with only subtle mention of producing a false negative result and another that makes overt claims about its products' intended purpose of subverting drug tests. The former, however, clearly dominates the market in advertising, in shelf space in retail shops, and in sales. Its presence is far more visible within traditional shopping venues. Its products are sold largely in retail shops. Those companies that make overt claims most commonly move their products from their Internet websites. The two types of detox company are explicated later in this chapter. First, however, it is necessary to describe the history of detox efforts before detoxification became an industry.

The Rise of the Detox Industry

For years prior to the takeoff of this rapidly expanding industry, individuals left to their own devices and volition concocted numerous substances and devised various procedures for purging drugs and concealing their use. An early study with heroin addicts and their efforts at duping urinalysis testing reported that 59 percent of the respondents described using flushing and substituting methods for producing false-negative test results (Lewis et al. 1973). Their diverse methods resulted in uneven degrees of success. Some do-it-yourself forms of subterfuge have proven effective at producing false negative results with EMIT tests. Simpler efforts, such as adding interfering substances to urine, have enjoyed less success, especially with the growth of advanced testing procedures such as the RIA and the GC/MS confirmatory procedures. Early yet less sophisticated methods of concealing drug use and producing false negative test results, in some cases, are still in use. Some of these methods may be effective even with sophisticated drug-detection procedures; others are little more than folklore.

Various personal or do-it-yourself strategies for duping drug tests, including abstinence, are still widely used. Regardless of the exact procedure of choice, the most commonly used methods are flushing, masking, substituting, and adulterating. Each is discussed below.

Widely known and propagated wisdom for beating urinalysis testing is to avoid providing the first urine of the day because it contains the highest levels of drug metabolites. Metabolite levels decrease across the day and are again at their highest the following morning, even if no additional drugs have been ingested. *Flushing,* or drinking large quantities of fluids prior to submitting a urine sample for drug testing, may accelerate the excretion of drug metabolites from one's system. This regimen reduces one's chances of having a positive drug test result. Over-the-counter diuretics,[1] coffee, tea, even beer are common ingestible drinks used for flushing. Each, after all, is a diuretic. As a result of flushing's proven success, the National Institute on Drug Abuse issued regulations limiting employees' water intake prior to their drug testing. Furthermore, flushing now can be detected by measuring a sample's creatine[2] and specific gravity—a process, however, that is costly and, as a result, infrequently used. Some employers' policies regarding on-site testing require that urine samples lacking color (an indication of flushing) simply be rejected. As a result, flushing proponents advise that about two hours prior to pissing on demand, individuals take B-complex vitamins, which give urine its distinctive hue. After all, a colorless urine sample raises suspicion, which can lead to further scrutiny: in some cases the outright rejection of a sample and in others, suspicion and continued monitoring of the person.

Masking, a vastly different strategy, is the ingestion of legal substances to cover up the presence of drug metabolites dispelled in urine. Individuals use everything from Tums and Rolaids to aspirin and ibuprofen in efforts at masking drug metabolites in urine. Some masking advocates recommend zinc sulfate (or the product Zinc Challenge). But with sophisticated technologies such as the GC/MS, confirmation tests normally detect and confirm ibuprofen and other masking agents.

Diluting the sample is another method that has been used with some degree of success. Diluting simply means adding water directly to the sample, which in turn theoretically dilutes the drug metabolites present in the urine. This chicanery largely was stymied during the Reagan administration's efforts at establishing drug-free work sites when former Attorney General Ed Meese ordered all federal toilets filled with blue dye. This prevented individuals from using water from toilet tanks to dilute their urine samples. Most currently used testing methods can yield immediate temperature readings, which is problematic for individuals diluting their sample with convenient water. As a result, diluting has become increasingly difficult to pull off and less successful than it once was as a method of duping drug tests.

Substituting is another method whereby one brings into the testing facility uncontaminated urine usually concealed in a condom or a bag specifically manufactured for this purpose (a bladder bag) and kept inside one's clothing. Some individuals obtain clean urine from nonusing friends (but we can only imagine the conversation). But, substitution as a ploy to produce a false negative result has become far more complex than when people simply relied on non-drug-using friends. Abbie Hoffman's final book, *Steal This Urine Test* (Hoffman and Silvers 1987), humorously mimicking his first publication's title, *Steal This Book,* highlights various methods of sabotaging employers' drug tests, from sleuth and shell games and rubber hoses with water bottles to the purchase of drug-free, freeze-dried urine for submitting as one's own. For a time, within the underground economy, drug-free, clean urine samples were marketed with prices ranging from fifty to five hundred dollars. Yet, subterranean entrepreneurs realized that urine has an unusually short shelf life (unless maintained in highly controlled conditions). Customers discovered that keeping the clean urine at normal body temperature and delivering it on demand posed a host of logistical problems. Today, newer innovative urine substitution procedures are used. For example, powdered urine is available from a Texas firm, Byrd Labs, founded by Jeffrey Nightbyrd, whose entrepreneurial spirit was documented in *Steal This Urine Test.* Byrd's powdered urine, according to directions, is to be mixed with water and maintained at body temperature until one offers it as one's own. Substitution, as a duping method, is less commonly used than previously.

An earlier Luddite tactic was to substitute urine with hydrochloric, sulfuric, or battery acid, which resulted in sabotaging testing mechanisms and equipment (Hoffman and Silvers 1987: 241). Of course, condoms, bladder bags, and plastic specimen cups could not maintain structural integrity when exposed to sulfuric or hydrochloric acids.

Adulterating samples by adding one thing or another to them also was more commonly used at one time than now. Adulteration is considered a successful strategy for deceiving drug-testing procedures and is still propagated within some drug-using subcultures. For example, adding liquid soap to urine reportedly results in a negative EMIT test result. Likewise, adding table salt and various cleaning agents allegedly has shown some degree of success. An old trick was to conceal table salt under one's fingernails, but federal guidelines now require subjects to wash their hands in the presence of a monitor before producing a urine sample (Potter 1999). Adding bleach or hydrogen peroxide, even in very small quantities, to a urine sample is widely believed to interfere with EMIT testing by decreasing the level of metabolites. The recent development and availability of inexpensive adulteration detection kits probably negates the use of these specific additives. (These detection devices are further discussed in chapter 4.) One particular product, UrinAid, an adulterant, is heralded as a successful additive, but, to the chagrin of some men and women in the armed forces, it will not fool RIA tests (i.e., those used by the military). UrinAid is available through Byrd Labs and the Butterfield-Jay Foundation of Oklahoma City.

Finally, some do-it-yourself tactics for subverting screening processes include mucking around with the paperwork that one must complete and sign prior to submitting to a drug test. Some claims also are made that inaccurate or incomplete paperwork will result in the rejection of a urine sample. For example, disruptive suggestions are to sign the wrong places, initial one place, mark through it, and initial elsewhere; and write in the area that clearly states "DO NOT MARK." When workers or applicants are tested, they typically are asked to provide information on any and all prescription and over-the-counter medication they have used during the previous seven days. This information is requested because many legal drugs have been confused for illicit ones. In other words, legal medications have produced false-positive test results. The requesting of such information is considered by many who object to drug testing as a further intrusion into their privacy. Employees and applicants often have good reason for not wanting their employer or prospective employer to be made privy to such sensitive information that, for many, is considered no one's business. Yet, in the main, employees and applicants comply for fear of being falsely accused. As a result, employers now have knowledge of who uses Lithium, Prozac, Percodan, AZT, Xanax, or any other legal drug whose use is highly personal and potentially publicly embarrassing (*Drug Testing: A Bad Investment* 1999). In response, some employees and applicants use this company coercion as a means of sabotaging the testing procedures. For example, when employers require information on any drug use during the previous seven days, some drug-testing subjects intentionally strike the word "seven" and write in "thirty" days. They then list every conceivable drug that has been known to cross-react with illicit drugs as a potential future defense if their sample results are returned as positive. (Greater attention to subversive behavior is detailed later on in this chapter and in chapter 5.)

In recent years, various pop-culture icons have published their own recipes for both beating drug tests and flushing toxins from one's body. That pop guru of holistic health, L. Ron Hubbard (1990), advanced his own detox plan (which on its face, and given the time required of individuals, seems impossible for working people): exercise and sauna for two to three weeks, five hours daily; run for thirty minutes, sauna for four hours, and get plenty of sleep; eat a healthy diet, drink plenty of water, and take two to four tablespoons of oil, niacin, and a special calcium and magnesium formula. His plan, like most published regimens, is guaranteed to flush out the impurities and yield a clean body and clear mind.

A 1981 publication advocating the benefits of herbal medicines and concoctions for ridding oneself of various toxins further advanced independent do-it-yourself efforts at self-cleansing or detoxing. Furthermore, it was an attempt at gaining ground for herbal remedies within orthodox medicine (Nebelkopf 1981). A most remarkable herbal tea—the Detox Brew—contained the herbs comfrey, spearmint, rosehips, orange peel, mullein, and goldenseal. The brew was recommended to addicts who were detoxing from opiates. The brew allegedly "acts as a tonic for the respiratory process and helps to remove the toxins from the body" (Nebelkopf 1981: 11). Detox Brew's last-listed ingredient—goldenseal—for centuries has been regarded as a natural cure-all that supposedly acts as a "tonic for the liver and kidneys in eliminating toxins from the bloodstream" (Nebelkopf 1981: 11). For decades, addicts who want to appear "clean on urinalysis tests for drugs" have used goldenseal although, as is discussed later in this chapter, there is little medical/scientific evidence of the herb's efficacy. Rather than goldenseal, the large quantity of fluids consumed prior to testing is the most logical explanation for the elimination of "toxins from the bloodstream" and the duping of urine-based drug-testing (Nebelkopf 1981: 65). Nebelkopf's point about ingesting large quantities of fluids with the herbal Detox Brew is especially salient. The ingestible products within the growing detox industry, which are addressed in greater detail in this chapter, also prescribe drinking large quantities of water.

Beyond Child's Play

Additional products and methods continually are propagated by their adherents and shared with increasing efficiency through various mediums. The recently developed and now widely used World Wide Web alone offers untold possibilities for advertising and selling products designed for subverting drug-testing procedures. The Internet apparently is the medium of choice for marketing products among the overt detox companies. It is at overt companies' websites where one finds obvious and stated uses for the detox wares—to beat drug tests.

Concentrated urine is available for purchase by ordering either directly from Clear Test, the manufacturer, or through various Internet sites. Clear Test's concentrated, drug-free urine is guaranteed to dupe any urinalysis testing, including both front-line (i.e., EMIT) and the more sophisticated confirmatory procedures, such as the GC/MS. The concentrated urine is advertised as adequate for two separate tests. Directions specify that the product be mixed with water (preferably in advance of when one is required to produce a specimen) and maintained at body temperature. Keeping urine at body temperature, for most people in most cases, is not a problem. But, given that Clear Test's urine is external to one's body, two distinct methods of keeping it warm are recommended: by one's own ingenuity or by using another product specifically designed for this purpose. Regarding the first, recommendations are made to store the liquid, drug-free urine in a condom under one's arm, inside one's pants, on one's inner thigh, or in a container (such as an Elmer's glue bottle) wrapped in hand warmers. The second method relies on the use of a far more sophisticated product—the Urinator. This device, which straps to one's upper thigh, stores the drug-free urine at body temperature and, powered by two nine-volt batteries, forces a stream of clean urine through a phallic-shaped prosthetic into a sample container. The benefit of the Urinator is that it is easily concealed and with charged batteries and clean urine can be used repeatedly. In fact, the advertising for the product boasts that it can be communally shared with others or, in an entrepreneurial spirit, rented to others. All one needs is a clean urine sample or Clear Test's concentrated urine product. Mystique's Optional Prosthetic Unit, designed to look and function like the real thing (for males, that is) is a comparable device. The downside is the Urinator's price—$150—but as advertisement boasts, the price can be offset if it is communally purchased.

Another method of subverting urinalysis testing is to surreptitiously add to the urine sample a product that is specifically designed to destroy all toxins and drug metabolites. Marketed by Clear Choice as Instant Clean Additive with a price of thirty dollars, claims include the following: it cannot be detected; it is pH balanced; it will neutralize even prescribed medications (which is a concern for people using some prescription drugs whether for medical or recreational purposes); and it will produce a false negative regardless of testing procedures. The additive is contained in a six-milliliter vial and comes with a double-the-money-back manufacturer's guarantee. The product may be especially useful to individuals subject to random testing.

Another additive product within the detox industry is UrinAid, which allegedly destroys drug metabolites in the sample. The manufacturer warns users, however, that it will not work with the RIA testing (the procedure used by the U.S. military).

These products—additives, concentrated urine, and the Urinator device—are far more sophisticated than earlier folk methods, procedures, and products. Unlike those earlier tactics, they depend on modern science and technology. Yet, they represent only a small segment of the newly emerging detox business, which offers a copious number of products and now comprises a multi-million-dollar industry. This detox industry's existence, emergence, and growth were not conceivable just a few short years ago. The dynamics of contemporary politics, moral campaigns, employment, economy, and law probably explain the origin and development of an industry, such as this, that manufactures and sells products to customers desiring to subvert legal and widely used drug-screening processes. The detox industry, as data show, is essentially two industries, one guarded or subtle and the other direct or overt. The former is composed of companies whose manufactured detox products are but one part of their manufacturing and sales. Such companies also market, for example, minerals, vitamin supplements, herbal remedies, and imported cigars, which are far more financially lucrative than their detox products. These companies are guarded about their detox products and cautiously advertise by using the most subtle language imaginable. The other type, the overt or direct companies, typically manufacture and sell only detox products. Their advertising is frank. They state in no uncertain terms that their products are designed to help consumers "beat drug tests." By comparison, the subtle companies advertise their products on their websites, in retail shops, and through word of mouth while the overt companies advertise on their websites and in the marijuana connoisseurs' periodical, *High Times* (among other media). Both types of manufacturing companies, however, sell essentially the same products. The difference is their methods. The subtle companies make up the vast majority of the detox business largely because they contract with wholesalers who place their products in retail shops and initiate contact with retail merchants. The overt variety typically sells directly to consumers who place orders by telephone or via the Internet. As a result, the bulk of this chapter focuses on the less conspicuous type of detox company that dominates the detox industry, with some attention given to the overt variety as well.

Subtle Sales

Several companies manufacture a wide assortment of detox products and sell them by using less obvious language than those companies that make conspicuous claims about their products and purpose. Those firms comprising the subtle variety include (1) Freedom Wholesalers in Mesa, Arizona, (2) Houston International of Tempe, Arizona, (3) Sarken of Tempe, Arizona, (4) Herbal Clean of Dublin, Ohio, (5) Vale Enterprises of Denver, Colorado, (6) One Source of Lake Bluff, Illinois, and (7) Clear Choice (Health Tech) of Alpharetta, Georgia. These companies and a few others like them market similar items with parallel claims of efficacy. Products include (1) herbal teas that detox in two hours, (2) pills that detox within two hours, (3) a bottled liquid that detoxes within one hour (which is the most popular detox item), (4) a freeze-dried powder designed for mixing with water and drinking, which detoxes in two hours, (5) daily cleansing capsules for continual detoxing, and (6) shampoos that eliminate toxins from hair within ten minutes.

More specifically, listed below is a sample of the less obvious companies and their products:

- Detoxify READY CLEAN, a liquid, is packaged in a sixteen-ounce bottle. Marketed as "easy and convenient," it is designed for the consumer to drink at least one hour prior to testing and "you're clean." The product's claim is that one is clean for up to five hours after consumption. Company advertising claims it is "the Number 1 seller in the industry." Price: $29.95.

- Detoxify XXTRA CLEAN "is a clinically-proven cleansing formula for people with higher toxin levels or larger body mass." Directions stipulate that the XXTRA CLEAN liquid should be mixed with "the powerful Concentrated Herbal Activator and it's guaranteed to work in one hour and be effective up to five hours." Price: $44.95.

- Detoxify FAST FLUSH CAPS, in capsule form, "is the perfect choice when you need a discreet cleansing formula that's easy to carry, anywhere you go." The capsules are designed to work in just one hour and effects last up to five hours. Price: $29.95 for twelve capsules.

- Detoxify CARBO CLEAN + PLUS "is formulated with ingredients known to assist the body's natural cleaning system." This product is designed for those who have the luxury of preparing for their test two to three days in advance. It includes PRECLEANSE CAPS, PRECLEANSE TEA, and CARBO CLEAN, a drink that is available in "3 delicious flavors." Price: $49.95.

- Detoxify CONSTANT CLEANSE. "Available in easy-to-take capsules, CONSTANT CLEANSE assists the body's natural detoxification process when used on a daily basis." It is designed to supplement other cleansing products for maximum detoxification. Price: $19.95 for a bottle of eighty capsules.

- Several "hair test solutions" or shampoos are available for producing false-negative hair-test results. The three most readily available are Herbalized Solutions' AFTERBURNER, Clear Choice's HAIR FOLLICLE SHAMPOO, and TOX-OUT SHAMPOO. The products claim that the shampoo "removes all residues and toxins within 10 minutes. Treatment lasts for up to 8 hours." Prices range from $35.00 to $149.00.

- Clear Choice QUICK FLUSH CAPSULES are designed to flush "all unwanted toxins in under 3 hours" and contain "vitamin B-complex and creatine." Price: $20.00.

- Clear Choice CARBO CLEANSING SHAKES are advertised as a "16 oz. ready-to-drink mix; just add water! Non fat chocolate or vanilla—No artificial ingredients." Price: $25.00.
- Clear Choice INSTANT CLEAN ADD-IT-IVE, a solution that is added to urine, allegedly "destroys all toxins on contact!" Claims are made that it is "laboratory tested—undetectable & pH balanced!" Price: $30.00.
- Clear Choice also markets liquid drinks that apparently are similar to Detoxify products. These drinks work in one hour and are effective for up to five hours. They are available in banana-berry, watermelon, piña colada and cran-apple cocktail flavors. Price: $24.95–$29.95.
- Clear Test, of Tohnert Park, California, a clearing house for various drug-detoxification products and books (such as *Ur-ine Trouble: The Truth about Drug Tests*; *Steal This Urine Test*; and *Conquering the Urine Test*) on subverting drug testing and the war on drugs, also markets an on-site testing kit designed to detect the presence of drugs in human urine. Testing time takes about ten minutes. Clear Test's website, where one can order any of the abovelisted items, reassures its customers that "for your privacy, credit card orders will be charged as 'books etc.' Products are shipped quickly and discreetly."
- MD Labs produces and distributes NATURALLY CLEAN, an herbal tea advertised as a detoxifier. MD also manufactures and distributes a product marketed for women—DAILY DETOX.
- Houston International markets a powder in a sixteen-ounce bottle designed for mixing with water, named THE STUFF, which is used for flushing toxins from one's system.
- BNG Enterprises manufactures and sells Herbal Clean products that include QUICK TABS, LIQUID CARBO, QUICK CARBO, and MASTER TEAS (ranging in price from $13.95 to $29.95). Each is advertised as a quick method of "flushing."
- Vale Enterprises manufactures and markets a powdered drink mix that works in two hours and whose effects last for five hours. Vale also manufactures ONE HOUR FORMULA, a liquid drink in grape, cherry, lemon, and orange flavors; ALL NATURAL HERBAL TEA, which will flush in two to three hours; PERMA-CLEAN capsules that offer a fifteen-day protection; and

DAILY CLEANSING FORMULA capsules that help the body with "continual cleansing."

- BODY FLUSH: THE MAXIMUM POTENCY TOXIN FLUSH, manufactured by Barnes Wholesale of Vencinnes, Indiana, is a liquid drink that works in one hour. Price: $20.00.
- HEAVEN SENT, quick capsules, are designed to eliminate toxins in one hour.
- CLEANZ BLENDZ, a detox tea manufactured by Basic Organics of Columbus, Ohio, is designed to flush toxins.
- General Nutrition Center, the national health store better known as GNC, sells a variety of detox products, including its own brand, DAILY CLEANSE CAPS. GNC's Quik Tabs, according to one manufacturer, is the industry's "biggest profit making item."

Apart from the abovelisted products, companies' promotional literature is filled with creative advertising claims and assurances for those doubting, yet potential, customers. For example:

- "Detoxify products are over 99% effective in the rapid removal of toxins."
- "Question: How do I know that Detoxify products work? Answer: You can trust Detoxify Brand products . . ."
- "The body can become less efficient at removing accumulated waste and toxins. This build up has been linked to reduction in energy levels and decreased natural defenses."
- "Detoxify: Your body's best defense against life's dirty little unpleasantries."
- "Ready Clean does not discriminate against the toxins it removes from the system."
- "Detoxify brand . . . is formulated with ingredients known to assist the body's natural cleaning system."
- "Ready Clean eliminates unwanted toxins."
- "Precleanse assists in lowering the level of toxins."

Nowhere in the detox products' literature or packaging, or in the advertising of companies of the subtle variety, will one find any mention of the products' intentions or alleged ability to flush or mask illegal drugs. Also, nowhere in the subtle companies' literature will one find anything about drug testing or meeting drug-screening deadlines. Drug use and testing, per se, are never mentioned. Yet, these manufacturers cautiously word their promotional materials to convey, however subtly, that the products are designed to help individuals pass drug tests. Consider the following instructions, for example:

- "The best time to meet the deadline is exactly 2 to 3 hours after drinking the bottle of Ready Clean." (Translation: Drink this two to three hours before having to piss on demand.)
- "For the period 48 hours prior to the deadline, avoid introducing toxins into the body." (Translation: At least two days before your drug test, stop smoking dope.)
- "Stay away from environments with heavy toxic smoke in the air." (Translation: Don't go to pot parties.)
- "Using Carbo-Drink as part of a complete detoxification program will assure you that you will be clean when you need to be clean." (Translation: This will enable you to pass the drug test.)
- "It is highly recommended that you begin taking Fast Flush Caps 90 minutes to 3 hours prior to the deadline." (Translation: If you want to pass the drug test, don't take this stuff too early or too late.)
- Houston International's products include the disclaimer that they "do not approve of or promote illegal drug usage. Naturally Klean was developed to protect the American Citizen from inaccurate testing, not to protect users of illegal drugs." (In the words of an industry spokesman, "This is legalese.")

As can be seen, no mention of drug use, drug testing, or testing deadlines appears in these products' instructions.

As a group, the subtle type of manufacturer is highly guarded when discussing its wares with outsiders, such as myself, who are interested in learning about products' composition, efficacy, distribution, and sales. This phenomenon provides an interesting comparison to my previous research, which relied on samples of individuals engaged in drug trafficking and property crimes. Detox manufacturers, compared to street criminals, were far more guarded and suspicious about my intentions. Many attempts to interview them were made, but with only limited success. They simply do not want outsiders raising questions about their products, their manufacturing, and their distribution. They are highly proprietary and overtly suspicious. They are insulated by the very names of their businesses, which usually are ambiguous and innocuous and reveal little about just what transpires within the four walls. Names such as BNG, Sarken, One Source, and Houston International could easily be used for a variety of businesses, from trucking to silicon chips. They also enjoy layers of insulation from outsiders, typically beginning with the most efficient of guardians—the company secretary. A March 1999 telephone call to one manufacturer is illustrative of the suspicion and insulation. A secretary answered.

> Q: May I speak with someone in a management position?
> A: About what?

I identified myself and explained why I needed to speak with someone other than her.
> A: Why?

I explained again.
> A: Hold please.

A minute later.

> A: There's no one here to talk with you.
> Q: Well, I don't want to talk at length with someone on the phone. I wanted to talk just a minute or two to introduce myself and explain what I'm doing. Then perhaps I could come up to Chicago and talk with them in person, if they would be willing.
> A: Hold please.

A minute later.

> A: There's no one here to talk with you. Can I take your name and number and have someone call you?
> Q: No, I'll call back. Who should I ask for?
> A: You know, I don't know who to tell you.
> Q: Well, what's your name?
> A: Lisa.
> Q: Well, I'll call back and ask for you.

Later in the day, I called back and talked with Lisa about a contact person there.

A: You know, I've asked and no one is interested in doing an interview or talking with you.

Q: Well, I'm surprised. Can you tell me why?

A: I really don't know. Sorry about that.

Later, I called back a third time, hoping that Lisa, who despite her secretarial status was serving as a very determined gate keeper, would be away from the phone, perhaps out of the office having lunch. Luckily, she was and I spoke with another secretary who directed me to a scientist on staff, Ronald. I left him a message. A few days later and after not having heard from Ronald, I called back. Lisa, of all people, answered the phone.

Q: Ronald, please.

A: May I tell him who's calling?

Q: Dr. Tunnell. I'm returning his call.

A: Who?

In part, manufacturers' reluctance to talk with anyone raising questions about their highly proprietary enterprise is explained by their previous encounters with members of the media. Manufacturers have been the subject of investigative television and newspaper reporting, which has had potentially adverse impacts on their business. Consider the following telephone conversation with a manufacturer in Phoenix.

A We are in the media all the time and this is a very touchy issue. You could be a media person misrepresenting yourself.

Q: Yes, I understand. But that's why I just wanted to talk a minute or two on the phone to touch base with you and then hopefully come to see you and meet you face to face. At that time we hopefully can talk at greater length. If you'd be willing.

(Telephone Interview, March 1999).

Manufacturers' reluctance undoubtedly is due also to their trading in products that reside in the gray area of legitimacy, that are the subject of investigative reporting, and that currently are prohibited in a few states. Manufacturers are on the defensive perhaps because they walk a thin line, claiming their products are for legitimate health care on the one hand, yet on the other hand marketing them so that there is little mistaking their

intended use—to produce false-negative urinalysis (and hair) testing results.[3]

Some manufacturers are more obvious than others about the intended
purpose of their products. For example, the overt variety (which is described later in this chapter), particularly those advertising in the marijuana connoisseurs' periodical *High Times,* openly makes claims about
their product's ability to beat drug tests. They also make these claims on
their company websites. Other manufacturers, specifically companies of
the subtle variety that also make products unrelated to detoxing, are less
conspicuous about the detoxing ability of their wares. These companies
produce consumer products completely unrelated to detoxing. In fact,
detox products comprise only a small part of the companies' annual profits (Private Interview with a detox company president, November 1999).
Consider how one Phoenix company spokesman of the subtle variety explained his products to me.

> Understanding that we're not in the modem of beating drug tests, we're
> just a detoxifier. With Naturally Clean, we present our product as a
> cleansing product versus a product to try to eliminate or try to beat drug
> testing. We also have a product called Daily Detox which is formulated
> for women, for detoxifying properties. But it also is definitely just some-
> thing for their . . . it's more considered for a kidney and liver cleansing.
> It is predominantly for health care, better health care. (Private Interview,
> September 1999)

Or another manufacturer, defending the company's veiled references to
beating drug tests, ultimately admitted that the company's language is
purposeful yet cautious:

> *A:* We do not condone drug use. The company's position is that these
>   products are not marketed for flushing illegal drugs.

I show him the language in the company literature that I had downloaded
from their website.

> *Q:* Given that drugs are not condoned and given the language such
>   as, "It will get you clean when you need to be clean," how does
>   your company reconcile the two?

A: This is probably just legalese

(Private Interview, March 1999)

Or two others:

A: We are opposed to drug use. Our products rid one of all unwanted toxins. For example, I had a cup of [detoxing] tea this morning. I sip on it across the day. It's for all kinds of uses. Women who are menstruating use it too. You need to detox from just the air you breathe in. It's a really good product.

(Private Interview, March 1999)

A: Our products do not mention drug use or that they're for flushing drugs. But about 80 percent of our customers use them for that. I even smoke a bit myself and see nothing wrong with it or with an employee using our products to keep his job. I use the tea on a near-daily basis to flush my system. [He gave me some samples.] We also make caps that will flush someone in one hour. People even carry them in their pockets.

(Private Interview, May 1999)

It is difficult to imagine why anyone detoxing solely for health benefits would feel the need to detox within an hour's time or carry in his or her pocket drugs producing that level of detox. There are exceptional or emergency cases, of course, for example, when individuals exposed to toxins in the workplace may need to detox as quickly and efficiently as possible. However, those are exceptional cases that are addressed by medical emergency personnel.

Another detox company spokesperson claimed that if he owned a company, he would drug test his employees. When asked about this he intimated that he is not necessarily opposed to drug use. Rather, he stated that there are a number of ways, including using his company's products, to pass a drug test. For him drug testing measures something else. In his words, "drug testing is more like an IQ test. If you can't pass a drug test, you're just stupid" (Private Interview, February 2003).

Company representatives are proprietary about the business of their business, or the process of manufacturing and selling their products. They are reluctant to provide any information that they define as proprietary. For example, the following response is indicative.

Q: Do you folks manufacture the products there in Tempe?
A: Sir, we don't give up our sources.

I inquired with another about the marketing of their product. The company spokesperson had let me know that their company's distributors are responsible for selling to wholesalers. Notice the cautious proprietorship in the following:

Q: Is there any way that you could put me in contact with the distributors?
A: With a distributor?
Q: Yes, that you folks work with.
A: I don't know if it would be to our benefit doing that. If you could give me a number, I can ask the distributors to call you.
Q: That would be great.
A: I just don't know if they would be comfortable being referred by me.

(Private Interview, April 1999)

I supplied my phone number. The call never came.
Consider another:

Q: Can you tell me how your products work?
A: No, I'm not going to tell you how our products work or what's in them.

(Private Interview, November 1999)

Companies that produce these products for flushing toxins have far more similarities than dissimilarities. The one most significant difference is that most of the companies described here are discreet about the specific use of their products while other companies publicize the specific intention of their anti-drug-testing wares. Those mentioned in this section are cautious with advertising language on websites and in their products' packaging; they also are guarded when talking with outsiders as they attempt to distance themselves from those who are more obvious about their products' intended use. Such differences are further illustrated later in this chapter when the conspicuous or overt firms are described. But, the next section on the retailing of detox products shows that shop owners and clerks are well informed about their products and the way consumers use them. Retailers at times are like manufacturers, discreet about the products' actual and intended use. Others, however, are far more honest and forthcoming than manufacturing spokespersons.

Retail Shops

Apart from manufacturers' websites, in the main detox products are sold in various retail stores, including health-food, dietary-supplement, and "head" shops. As a group, retailers sell at least one detox product daily, and on some days several items, such as when a local business is about to initiate random testing or hire new employees (and thus drug screen applicants). Although random testing supposedly is unannounced, proprietors claim that employees, as has been explained to me, nearly always hear about such at least a couple of days beforehand. For example, a proprietor of one head shop had sold ten units of a product the day that I talked with him. Evidently, employees of a local manufacturing plant had learned that the company was about to initiate random testing. That particular proprietor, who happily profited from sales, was oddly critical of the products and defined them as a "waste of money." According to him, it is the *process* itself described in the products' instructions rather than the *products* that generate false-negative test results. For example, nearly every detox product recommends flushing or drinking large quantities of water for several days in advance of the deadline (if possible), abstaining from ingesting other toxins, avoiding toxic environments, urinating frequently, and eating a considerable amount of fruits and vegetables—all commonsense recommendations. It was his opinion that those measures are sufficient in themselves and that the products he sells are unnecessary. He also slipped me his home remedy for detoxing: follow the abovementioned commonsense procedures (absent a detox product) and one hour prior to the deadline, drink a bottle of Nestles chocolate milk, whose lactase coats the cells and masks the toxins.

Retail proprietors' responses to my interest and queries ranged from openness to guarded suspicion. But, in each case, they clearly articulated that they recognize that detox products are used by desperate individuals hoping to beat drug tests. Yet most also claimed that they avoid talking

Newspaper advertisement for detox products (among others).

about such uses with their customers and instead speak only of the products' ability to mask and flush toxins rather than illicit drugs. Customers, however, make it clear to them just how they intend to use their products.

One locally owned nutritional retail shop located in a city of 250,000 people has been owned by a husband and wife team for more than twenty years (although as of this writing, it is no longer in business). In addition to the nutritional items stocking the simple wooden shelves, they boldly display and sell (and advertise in a local newspaper) "white crosses" (bronchial dilators that contain a healthy dosage of a stimulant). A few years ago, the retail shop expanded its inventory and began selling herbal products and vitamins. During the past nine years the store has advertised and sold detox products (viz., Naturally Klean and Herbal Clean). According to the owners with whom I talked, a representative from Sarken of Tempe, Arizona, telephoned them about the company's detox products; soon afterwards they began doing business with Sarken. The retailers claim to sell at least one detox product per day to customers whom they typify as casual marijuana users. When I pointed out that none of the products' packaging mentions drug use or eliminating drugs to beat drug tests, the owner agreed with my observation. She then stated that she and her husband also refrain from talking of drug use with customers and instead discuss with them the products' abilities at flushing toxins (Private Interview, October 1998).

A few months later, and in another state, I visited a locally owned head shop that not only sells innovative smoking paraphernalia but also compact discs, incense, incense burners, and metal bands' T-shirts. According to the owner, he discovered detox products while surfing the Internet and was later contacted by One Source, the company that manufactures and markets Detoxify products. The owner claims that the shop does business solely with One Source and places orders with them by using a company catalog. According to the owner, "Other manufacturers call me, but I just deal with this one company. They're easy to deal with." Although sales admittedly are erratic, the owner happily reported that they sell large numbers of the products in a town of only twenty-seven thousand inhabitants.

A: I'll tell you one thing about this product, we sell buckets of it.

Q: What do you mean by buckets?

A: A thousand units in the past year, and that's a conservative estimate.

Q: And this product sells for what?

A: Twenty bucks. I don't know how it works, but I've heard it flushes and I've heard it masks. So, I don't know. But it must work. We've had three people in the past year want a refund. One guy said that he had burned a number on the way to the piss test and failed. I said, "Man, you shouldn't be doing smoke anyway, and especially right before a piss test." You see, I think that herb ought to be legal. I hate to say that, and I'm careful who I say it to, but there are good reasons for it. It's not as harmful as, for example . . . where are my cigarettes?

(Private Interview, August 1999)

I visited a locally owned health food store in a town with a population of eight thousand. The town is dominated by a religious but nondenominational Protestant college. When asked if they carry detox products, the clerk replied, "Yes. They're behind the counter." She indicated that they believe it best, given the conservative, Protestant worldview of the town, to discreetly sell detox products. She showed me her wares: Detoxify— the liquid, the capsules, and a daily detox. Although they at one time sold other brands, they carry only Detoxify now because, according to the clerk, "this company is very good to do business with. We just phone in our orders." She has worked in the store for two years and during that time they have sold at least one product per day. I inquired if they are ever offered a reason for customers' purchasing these products. She replied, "Drug testing. Either a company is doing testing or a company is hiring and testing applicants" (Private Interview, October 1998).

When entering another health food store, I saw there were no customers as the proprietor greeted me. We had the following conversation:

Q: Do you carry any detox products?
A: Like stuff for drug tests?
Q: Yeah.
A: Yeah, we have four or five products.
Q: Do you sell many of these?
A: Oh yeah. Lots. Well, some every day.

(Private Interview, May 1999)

In this case, the shop keeper, without having been asked, volunteered that, according to his understanding, the products are designed to aid in passing drug tests. Of the various retail merchants interviewed for this study, he was among the least guarded.

In contrast to his openness, another shopkeeper in a health and mineral supplement retail shop was unwilling to discuss the issues at any length.

Q: Do people ever say what they want with these products?
A: No. That's pretty much understood. They know what they're looking for when they come in.
Q: Do you sell a lot?
A: I don't want to say. You should talk with the manager.

(Private Interview, May 1999)

In an ethnically mixed middle-class area of a city of 250,000 people, I talked with the owner of a locally owned store that sells health foods, organic cosmetics, and supplements. The owner certainly understood and articulated the purpose of her products.

Q: Do you carry detox products?

A. Yeah, just one. [She pulls a closed wooden box measuring about two feet square from behind the counter, opens it, and pulls out a bottle.] This is THE STUFF, liquid that doesn't flush, it masks.

Q: It masks?

A: Yeah, it conceals the presence of drugs. When's your test?

Q: I don't know.

A: We've carried it for five years. This really works, but it's expensive—$29.99.

(Private Interview, May 1999)

My discussions with retail merchants about these products took me to several stores that are part of the national chain General Nutrition Center (GNC). Each GNC stocks a variety of detox products, such as BNG's QUIK CAPS and, perhaps unbeknownst to many of GNC's regular shoppers, GNC's own DAILY CLEANSE CAPS, designed for flushing toxins. One store manager and I had the following conversation about GNC's policies and participation in selling items used for subverting drug-testing procedures:

A: GNC has to approve all products sold in GNC stores, so they are selective. As a result, whenever manufacturers call a particular store advertising their products, they cannot accept unless the central office has.

Q: Do you sell many of these products?

A: It depends on the socio-demographics of where a particular store is located. For example, here in the west [an upscale area] we don't sell very many, not one per day. But, at the Clinton store [a working-class area] they sell lots more.

Q: When people come in to buy them, do they ever say what their purpose is?

A: Yeah, sometimes. But, even if they don't, you can tell. A lot of people act real paranoid and others ask if the product is guaranteed for them to pass a drug test. I tell them that they come with a money-back guarantee, but that no one product will absolutely work on everyone. People have different metabolisms.

(Private Interview, May 1999)

These products are sold in a variety of retail shops, from the out-of-the-way head shop to the national franchise, GNC. Retailers, with the exception of one, condemned drug use although each retailer was well aware of the purpose of the products. While condemning drug use, they nonetheless felt uncompromised by selling a product designed to negate a type of social control—drug testing in the workplace. Although this situation constitutes a moral conundrum, retailers were able to stock and sell these products nonetheless. Their condemnation on the one hand and willingness to sell on the other may seem odd on its face. Yet, such behavior is similar to store clerks who may be opposed to smoking cigarettes yet who nonetheless sell dozens of cartons per day; liquor store clerks who condemn excessive drinking yet easily sell cases of beer and gallons of liquor to a single customer; or a vegan grocery store clerk who may spend her days wrapping pound after pound of ground beef and sausage links. Retailers down the line, and in a variety of businesses, have proven able to reconcile the incompatible (and sometimes unethical or illegal) qualities of their work with their ideologies (see, e.g., Blumberg 1989). Retailers in the detox industry are no different. Perhaps, at least in some cases, retailers use techniques of neutralization—mechanisms that help them rationalize their behavior while engaged in the process of selling and neutralize deviant or inferior images of themselves afterwards (see, e.g., Sykes and Matza 1957).

Industry Trade Shows

The majority of manufacturing firms of the subtle variety produce items other than detox products. These additional commodities often include muscle-building drugs, athletic drinks, diet regimens, dietary supplements, minerals, and vitamins. One company imports Caribbean cigars. The hinge pins that link manufacturers, wholesalers, and distributors to retailers are industry trade shows.

Trade shows within the larger dietary, mineral, and supplement industry, held several times yearly and in a variety of locations, are most often connected to the national organization, National Nutritional Foods Association (NNFA). An NNFA spokesperson, during a phone conversation, claimed that the organization's mission is to link manufacturers with retailers through various NNFA-related trade shows and to lobby Congress about federal regulation of industry products.

> It's basically an organization of retail health food stores and outlets and for the natural food and supplements in the vitamin industry. So, lobbying Congress and alternative medicine. The trade shows are usually the exhibitors, they are the manufacturers of these products and of course they hold it for the retail store owners to come to find things to put on their shelves. There are [also] legislative efforts. I mean the organization does things besides trade shows. Which is again lobbying, trying to get better regulations about the foods and supplements to keep the FDA from cracking down too hard. That's one of the missions of the organization. (Private Interview, April 1999)

The annual national meeting is usually held in Las Vegas and in July (of all times). Regional meetings are held in various cities throughout the year. Some regional conferences (particularly those on the East Coast) are organized and administered by New Hope Natural Media, a division of Penton Media. Located in Boulder, Colorado, New Hope publishes a number of health, science and food periodicals. It also produces Natural Products Expo (East and West), an exposition of manufacturers' goods and products, such as natural foods, supplements, and vitamins.

NNFA convention activities are varied, seeming to offer something for everyone. Workshops and seminars dominate the meeting but the most common theme is advancing the industry and its products. The following topics were published as part of one recent meeting's agenda: Research in Cancer Prevention and Treatment; Homeopathy; Antioxidant Research; Food Operations; Herbs for the Next Millennium; Food-Supplement Connection; Your Health Is Skin Deep; Claims for Functional Food; No More Amoxicillin; The Osteoporosis Solution; and Herbals vs. Pharmaceuticals. Supporting the NNFA spokesperson's claims about the organization's mission of lobbying and countering regulatory law, at least a couple of seminar topics focus on the industry and regulation—Regulatory Oversight and Washington Update seminars. Although the products themselves comprise the primary subject of the various seminars, industry concerns, marketing, retailing, and profit maximization also receive significant coverage. For example, some seminar topics include Marketing Food/Dietary Needs; Competitive Marketplace; The XYZs of Retail Selling; Recruiting and Hiring; Industry Trends/Competition; Increasing Store Profitability; Ad Strategies That Soar; Sharpening Your Retail Edge; International Trade; and Bringing in the Masses. National Nutritional Foods Association's meetings also offer several health-related activities for conference participants such as yoga, aerobics, a 5K run and a 2.5K walk. Each convention has a keynote speaker including news-reading celebrity John Stossel, ABC's *20/20* correspondent, whose address was titled *Pandering to Fear: The Media's Crisis Mentality*. The NNFA also offers participants a distance learning program whereby one can earn an Associate of Science degree, by way of independent study, in applied nutrition.

During earlier conversations with two different spokespersons whose companies manufacture detox products (among other nutritional and supplemental items), I was informed that detox products are displayed at both national and regional industry trade shows. These individuals work for companies that are part of the discreet branch of the detox industry. Upon their advice, and using a bogus business card to gain admission, I attended the 15th Annual Natural Products Expo East trade show in Baltimore during October 1999. With 350,000 square feet of trade show floor space and 1,728 exhibitor booths, the convention made professional academic conferences look bush league. The exhibitors included 22 international; 167 certified organic; 118 personal care; 45 specialty foods; 18 vegetarian; 129 vitamins/supplements; and 22 environmental booths. As with the NNFA meetings described above, the Natural Products Expo East offered seminars on industry products, marketing tactics, and political initiatives for evading and revising government regulation. The regional meeting also featured keynote speakers (including several Ph.D.s) across the four days.

As I meandered through the convention hall, with a microcassette recorder discreetly tucked away, I dictated field notes whenever opportunity presented itself. That was not always easy, for the place was swarming with private security. The hired guards were engaged in a number of activities but mostly were simply staring at conventioneers to ensure they wore the appropriate credentials. Posing as a retail merchant and thus equipped with an approved name tag, I strolled along unencumbered by security (whom I saw turn the uncredentialed away). The following is a part of my dictated field notes, verbatim:

Credentials are an amazing thing. Because of my name tag, I have carte blanche to enter any door, to pick up company literature (which is abundant), to sample products, and to pass with complete freedom through exhibition space. They know nothing else about me other than what this name tag says. It's a unidimensional assumption about people and speaks volumes about the power of master status. (Field Notes, October 22, 1999)

Then, later, while walking through the bustling convention exhibition hall, I witnessed and overheard two individuals dressed in white laboratory coats. Desperately trying to look very medical-doctor-like, they were hawking their wares by barking out the outrageous claim that their product "prevents breast cancer." An individual working another booth held high a book in one hand and loudly announced, "Here's one I just wrote." I couldn't help but imagine such carny tactics at academic conferences (Field Notes, October 22, 1999).

As I wandered through the maze of 350,000 square feet of exhibitors' space, it soon became obvious that every person staffing a convention booth possessed similar physical characteristics. Again, from my field notes:

The people who work booths, to generalize, are beautiful. Young, fit, trim, well tanned, they appear to be the perfect image of health.

Yet, later, at an outdoor café just across the street from the convention center, several convention-goers gathered for lunch. A surprising number smoked cigarettes and looked disheveled, pasty, too well-fed, and far from fit. The distinction was striking. The image of corporate workers pushing their "health" products as perfect specimens of natural health and beauty easily led to the conclusion that the most obvious difference between them and the overfed conventioneers was that the former used the products they hawked while the latter did not. Advertising certainly promotes that assumption as health and fitness are now sold in a capsule (Field Notes, October 22, 1999).

Walking through the exhibit area for an entire day, looking at each exhibit and the products on display, I saw, however, a grand total of two booths with detoxing and flushing products. Those booths were representing the very two manufacturers whose spokespersons advised me to attend the convention. Promotional literature on the Natural Products

Expo West (another regional organization) convention indicates likewise—detox manufacturers are not there exhibiting their wares. It was only after attending and perusing other convention materials that I realized the bulk of the detox industry remains more subterranean than I had been led to believe by those two manufacturing spokespersons.

The spokespersons who advised my attending the conventions are employed with companies that manufacture numerous items, only some of which are detox or flush products. In fact, they sell far fewer detox items than any of their other product lines. Their companies are among the subtle variety. But, since they attend conventions, they may have had the impression that other manufacturers like them also attend. They attend trade shows promoting all of their products. The detox wares simply are a small part of their entire product line.

Those overt companies that manufacture only detox products are not likely to attend trade shows since they operate at the periphery of the vitamin/supplement industry and have no other product line to display. The conventions, after all, are representing an industry that is doing its very best to become further legitimized with the public and the state. Consider, for example, Natural Products Expo's statement of purpose regarding its standards program:

> Our goal is to enhance public health and safety, support industry self-regulation, and foster the responsible growth of our industry. We present these standards in a spirit of cooperation with current industry efforts to ensure quality and integrity. We also believe these standards will increase consumer confidence in products exhibited at our Expos.

Such statements clearly indicate efforts at legitimizing the industry, a mission that is incompatible with companies whose products are designed solely to help drug users subvert drug-testing policies and programs. The latter may actually have more in common with entrepreneurs selling online college term papers and hydroponic growing kits[4] than with an industry that is certified, that lobbies in Washington, and that holds several major conventions per year with thousands of attendees and exhibitors. These types of efforts are indicative of traditionally legitimate business maneuvers, unlike the operations of those companies that overtly sell drug-masking and flushing products with the stated use of negating drug tests. It is this overt variety that next receives attention.

Overt Detoxing Companies

The obvious detox companies comprise a small minority of the detox industry. Their sales tactics are dissimilar to widely recognized standard procedures of doing business. For example, this type of company does not use distributors, wholesalers, and retailers; it does not attend industry trade shows. This type of detox company makes blatantly unguarded statements about its products. For example, typical claims are that the products will "beat drug tests" or "produce false negative" results on drug tests. The overt type of company advertises and sells its products almost solely through its websites. The development of the World Wide Web clearly has led to the proliferation of numerous companies selling all manner of products, such as these, in a largely unregulated arena.

The following paragraphs describe a sample of company websites and products that are easily accessed. In fact, according to the *Washington Post* ("Firms offer ways" 2003) if one simply types "beat drug test" into an Internet search engine, more than one hundred websites will pop up.

The website passpee.com features a separate section titled "How to Beat a Drug Test." After offering abstinence as a solution and then counseling "light smokers" to flush using water with daily vitamin supplements "to re-color the dilute [*sic*] urine from the flushing effects," more detailed wisdom is offered for the "moderate smoker." Assuming this type of user incapable of passing unannounced random testing especially when using only a water-flushing method, the site advises use of a urine additive that "will destroy the THC metabolites, giving the appearance of drug free urine." If someone selected for random testing has an hour or two before having to piss on demand, passpee.com recommends using a "detoxifying carbodrink." The site recommends detoxifying drinks rather than urine additives because the former is consistent across products; additives, it is alleged, are not entirely reliable.

According to the passpee.com website, flushing teas, which depend on the ingestion of large quantities of water, are not supported by scientific research; "thousands of people," nonetheless, "have enjoyed repeated success with teas." The site cautions, however, that the "effect of the teas are [*sic*] seldom from the ingredients, the benefit is the gallon of water . . . the ingredients [are] irrelevant." This is similar to the wisdom volunteered by others interviewed who suggested that the product is a waste of money. Rather, it's all in the water. Carbo drinks are another matter.

Touted as "proven to work by the scientific community [and] extremely effective for the light to moderate smoker," carbo drinks "prevent the toxins from leaving the body."

Comedian/actor Tommy Chong, of the Cheech and Chong duo, for a time advertised his product, "Tommy Chong's Urine Luck," on the urineluck.com website. (He now has his own website that promotes only Tommy Chong productions at tommychong.com.) Using the bold advertising "Pass Any Drug Test—Guaranteed!" Chong's urineluck.com on-line ordering service offered, at thirty dollars per unit, Urine Luck, Quick Fix, Quick Fizz, Shampoo, Tommy Chong's Carbo Drink (in three flavors), Quick-Flush Capsules, and three flavors of Carbo-Tea Mix. The urineluck.com website currently is unrelated to Chong. Visiting the site today, one finds no mention of Chong; instead the site advertises Spectrum Lab Products with Spectrum Lab's Urine Luck. The new Urine Luck website not only offers various products of subterfuge but also on-site testing kits and a laboratory analysis (at forty-five dollars per). The Urine Luck product is a urine additive "designed for the daily user." Claims are made that the additive is "undetectable." The Carbo-Drink, also touted as "undetectable," is "designed for individuals who smoke four times a week or less."

Each of these advertised products is highly similar to the myriad available from manufacturers of the subtle variety. The notable difference is that this company, as is the case with all overt ones, clearly states that its products are designed to flush, mask, or negate drug metabolites and produce false-negative results. Further exemplifying the obvious purposes of these products, Spectrum Lab's website has an on-line test to determine which of its products is best suited for individuals and their varying levels of drug use. The home page of the site states, "To see what products suits [sic] your needs the best, take our interactive product selection test by clicking the button below." The button, a picture of a marijuana leaf, when clicked on sends up a message that asks the user to select the type of drug test. When "urine test" was selected, the following question appeared: "How many times a week do you smoke pot or take other substances?" Other links are posted at Spectrum's website, including links to the American Civil Liberties Union, marijuananews.com, and Pot Smokers of America.

Spectrum Lab's website offers the following products and product-specific directions: Urine Luck, an additive, "works on all toxins, including alcohol and tobacco. These toxins are all organically based so the

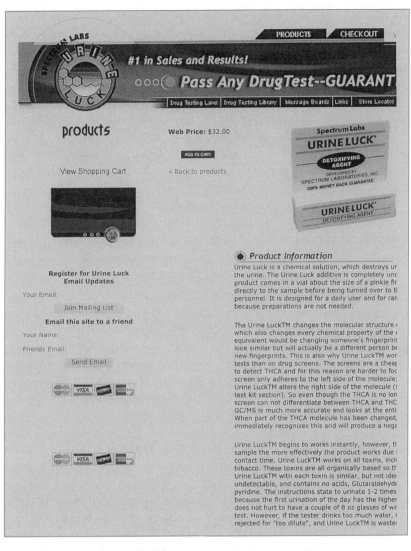

Spectrum Labs

#1 in Sales and Results!

○○○● **Pass Any DrugTest--GUARANT**

| Drug Testing Laws | Drug Testing Library | Message Boards | Links | Store Locator

products

Web Price: $32.00

ADD TO CART

View Shopping Cart « Back to products

Spectrum Labs

URINE LUCK®

DETOXIFYING AGENT

DEVELOPED BY
SPECTRUM LABORATORIES, INC.
200% MONEY BACK GUARANTEE

URINE LUCK®
DETOXIFYING AGENT

**Register for Urine Luck
Email Updates**

Your Email:

Join Mailing List

Email this site to a friend

Your Name:

Friends Email:

Send Email

● **Product Information**

Urine Luck is a chemical solution, which destroys ur
the urine. The Urine Luck additive is completely und
product comes in a vial about the size of a pinkie fin
directly to the sample before being turned over to tl
personnel. It is designed for a daily user and for ran
because preparations are not needed.

The Urine Luck™ changes the molecular structure
which also changes every chemical property of the
equivalent would be changing someone's fingerprint
look similar but will actually be a different person be
new fingerprints. This is also why Urine Luck™ wor
tests than on drug screens. The screens are a chear
to detect THCA and for this reason are harder to foc
screen only adheres to the left side of the molecule;
Urine Luck™ alters the right side of the molecule (
test kit section). So even though the THCA is no lon
screen can not differentiate between THCA and THC
GC/MS is much more accurate and looks at the entir
When part of the THCA molecule has been changed,
immediately recognizes this and will produce a nega

Urine Luck™ begins to works instantly, however, tl
sample the more effectively the product works due
contact time. Urine Luck™ works on all toxins, incli
tobacco. These toxins are all organically based so tl
Urine Luck™ with each toxin is similar, but not ider
undetectable, and contains no acids, Glutaraldehyde
pyridine. The instructions state to urinate 1-2 times
because the first urination of the day has the highe:
does not hurt to have a couple of 8 oz glasses of wa
test. However, if the tester drinks too much water, l
rejected for "too dilute", and Urine Luck™ is waste

Spectrum Labs' Urine Luck additive. *Courtesy of Spectrum Labs.*

mechanism of Urine Luck with each toxin is similar, but not identical. It is undetectable." According to the website's advertising claims, "Urine Luck has a 99.6 percent success rate at beating urine analysis if directions are followed." Spectrum Lab's website specifically claims that Urine Luck is designed for the "daily user and for random testing." While there might be something to these claims, the alleged scientific process of Urine Luck is a bit dubious. According to the website, Urine Luck "changes the molecular structure of the compound, which also changes every chemical property of the compound. The equivalent would be changing someone's fingerprints. They might look similar but will actually be a different person because they have new fingerprints." What?

Another innovative item of the overt variety is Bake-n-Shake, which is designed to remove toxins from the urine sample itself. Bake-n-Shake is a bag that an individual, while not being observed by a monitor, urinates into before transferring the sample into an approved sample container. Instructions are to urinate in the bag, shake it, and then pour the contents into the urine sample container. According to product advertising,

> Two chemicals are in the bag. One chemical destroys the toxins, while the second chemical destroys the first chemical. The compounds end up breaking down to air and water. The toxins remain in the bag and are discarded when the users throw the bag away. This product is perfect for the heavy smoker that needs to detoxify at a moment's notice. No traces of the product or toxins are left behind in the urine.

According to Spectrum Lab's claims, Carbo-Drink is designed for individuals who smoke four times a week or less. The Carbo-Drink is a

> detoxifying product that actually holds the toxins in your body. Toxins are stored in the fat cells of the body. For these toxins to be released the fat cells must be burned and the toxins are released in the blood stream. In the blood the toxins are filtered out by the kidneys and sent onto the bladder. The Carbo-Drink prevents the body from burning fat cells so the toxins are never released.

Spectrum's Quick Fizz allegedly works similarly, that is, it allegedly holds the toxins in the body, preventing them from being dispelled in urine. Designed for people who "smoke four times a week or less" the Quick Fizz effervescent tablets "dissolve easily in water and tastes [*sic*] great."

Spectrum also markets a bottle of premixed laboratory urine, sold as Quick Fix. Spectrum claims that the urine is "unisex so a male or female can use it. To ensure passing a urinalysis, the Quick Fix contains all the ingredients normally found in urine and is balanced for pH, specific gravity, creatine, and several other urine characteristics."

The website cleanwhizz.com evidently markets only "drug-free" urine. According to the site's promotional language, some customers "for a variety of reasons, need clean urine." The clean urine arrives in two nine-ounce bags along with a hose and hose clamp, four heat packs, two thermometers, and straps and attachments. According to the website, the clean urine should be kept warm and strapped to one's body with the hose fed through the legs to provide "everything you need to simulate the act of urination." Although there may indeed be a "variety of reasons" why an individual might "need clean urine," it is difficult to imagine many legitimate and scrupulous reasons as to why one would need to simulate urination.

The website passyourdrugtest.com features a number of high-end products reportedly designed by "master herbalists . . . [who] go out of their way to stay on top of current testing methods and develop kits to ensure a passing test result, every single time." The company markets urine, saliva, blood, and urine cleansers and hair-cleansing solutions for masking and flushing toxins. Also advertised are at-home self-test kits and urine additives. One promotional tactic advertised on the website is, "Purchase any of our permanent cleansing kits and receive two free self-test kits." For those seeking a method of beating drug tests, instructions are to "click here to see the different ways you can remove all toxins including marijuana from your blood and urine." Product prices range from $24.95 for Klear Carbo Drink, touted as "perfect for concert goers and very light users," to $99.00 for Never Fail Urine Cleanser, which is "perfect for daily users, no matter what you use," all the way up to $153.00 for All Drugs Follicle Cleanse, an "all drug removing shampoo kit" that is "perfect for those of you that partake in a little more than marijuana." The product making the most blatant claims is After Burner Hair Shampoo, which, according to the website, is "a revolutionary new way to rid the hair shaft of toxins such as THC (marijuana), cocaine, amphetamines, methamphetamines, opiates (heroin), etc." Passyourdrugtest.com, just like urineluck.com, posts a series of frequently asked questions and answers "to make sure you pass your drug test." The number of queries, or "hits," for each type of test (viz., urine, blood, saliva, hair) are posted as follows: urine—59,687; blood—6,671; saliva—2,006; and hair—6,184, for a total of 74,548 (as of February 12, 2002). As of April 10, 2003, the total number of hits was reportedly 270,443, a 362-percent increase.

Perhaps the most obviously titled website among the overt variety is beatanydrugtest.com. Logging on to the site one immediately sees, "Beat any drug test with Clear Choice Products." Clear Choice offers the usual assortment of detoxing products, each with a double-the-money-back guarantee.

Although 1stopdetox.com states that it "will not in any way, shape or form . . . cheat any drug screening or testing procedure," it advertises products explicitly designed for subverting drug tests. Its Master Chew, for example, is heralded as "a new technical breakthrough in the drug testing industry. This new product is a chewable tablet that was developed specifically to block THC from passing through the urine of the body. There is nothing like it in the industry, it is NOT a masking agent."

Testclean.com introduces its website visitors to its site with the greeting, "Pass the Urine Drug Test and Hair Drug Test with these products." Its products are typical for the industry: powdered urine, urine additive, Quick Caps, shampoo, and a sixteen-ounce drink.

Three clearing houses for overt detox products are perhaps the places where most desperate novices begin. Each website offers numerous links to specific overt companies offering essentially the same products. Detox-central.com, detoxking.com, and yahooka.com literally publish dozens of pages of advertising for a wide assortment of companies.

The marijuana connoisseurs' periodical, *High Times,* has at its website's home page an internal link to "Pot Reference." From there, visitors can peruse issues such as "Cultivation," "Market Quotes," and "Drug Testing." At "Drug Testing Information," readers are informed of *High Times*'s Drug Testing Hotline, which reportedly has "helped over 150,000 pass drug tests since [it] was founded in 1989." The advice, which *High Times* disclaims as legal, is sold similarly to phone sex or psychic advice at $1.95 per minute. The website's actual wording follows:

> HIGH TIMES does not advocate or condone cheating on drug tests or trying to dishonestly defeat urine, blood, hair or perspiration tests. The HIGH TIMES Hotline describes methods for obtaining passing results as TECHNICAL INFORMATION AND FOR EDUCATIONAL PURPOSES ONLY.

Manufacturers of the subtle variety of detox products believe that they and their business are tainted by the very presence of such overt drug products and advertising. One manufacturer compared his subtle advertising strategies to those companies making obvious assertions about their products.

> There are about eight big companies and then fifteen or so smaller ones. Those smaller ones say outright that their products flush drugs. They actually say that this will flush cocaine and this pot. You can see their ads in *High Times* and stuff in head shops. (Private Interview, May 1999)

Ironically, one typically finds the subtle rather than overt companies' products in head shops and health food stores. The overt variety tends to market its wares almost solely in *High Times* and through its websites.

Desperation, Gullibility, and Marketplace Deception

Paul Blumberg's (1989) richly detailed work reveals that deception, bait-and-switch tactics, and shortchanging consumers are normal practices among both industrial and service-sector businesses. Apart from the meticulous revelations of his work, Blumberg situates much of the ongoing duplicity within the context of modernity, increasing specialization, and advancing technological developments. Blumberg's thesis is that despite regulatory efforts to the contrary, marketplace deception and quackery, in many respects, have become much easier than was previously the case. Due to increasing sophistication of marketable products, slick advertising, and the endless array of meaningless choices, consumers have fallen further and further behind in their knowledge of the very products that they define as needs. The result is the opposite of a well-informed consumer; rather, "the prime feature of our age is actually the centrality of theoretical ignorance" (Blumberg 1989: 60). This translates into a sorry state for most consumers, as "the typical citizen knows less and less about more and more as technology soars beyond his capacity to understand" (Blumberg 1989: 60).

This condition is not due simply to the state of advanced societies. Among openly democratic societies that embrace the praxis of egalitarianism, information would be readily shared from expert to layperson. Such a process is, on its face, anti-elitist. But, such is not the case in predatory societies, where "public ignorance is useful to the expert." In this instance, "the more ignorant the public, the more dependent and powerless that public is at the hands of the expert and the more economically vulnerable" (Blumberg 1989: 75). The "technical complexity of modern life" within predatory societies has "made ignorance endemic, and hence many people simply abdicate their own judgement and passively put their lives in the hands of experts" (Blumberg 1989: 80).

Given this scenario and consumers' overwhelming desire to purchase quick fixes in a bottle or capsule, in hindsight the rise of an industry based on quick detoxing seems inevitable. Consumers, without question, trust the hocus-pocus of the magic elixir of detox products. The products after all are nicely packaged, littered with testimonials, and offer a 200- (in some cases 300-) percent money-back guarantee.[5] Furthermore, they are among the mysterious type of products—those largely used internally—of which consumers are highly uninformed. Consumers typically know more about the workings of their personal computers than of their own bodies. Thus, ignorance, gullibility, desperation, and predation are fundamental to the rise of this industry. But, these factors alone are not enough to account for the take-off of the detox industry. Government itself and the current state of regulation are central to the emergence and proliferation of this industry.

Health and herbal remedies and supplements were exempted from Food and Drug Administration (FDA) regulations through federal legislation in 1994 (viz., the Dietary Supplement Health and Education Act of 1994, Public Law 103-417). The FDA regulates dietary supplements under different regulations than those pertaining to traditional foods and drugs. Under FDA regulations, the dietary supplement manufacturers are responsible for ensuring that their products are safe before they are marketed. After these products reach the market, the FDA assumes responsibility for taking action against any unsafe supplement. Manufacturers are not required to register with the FDA or get the FDA's approval before producing or marketing dietary supplements. As a result of this deregulation, companies are free to claim nearly anything (other than disease treatment or prevention) about the efficacy of their products. While new FDA regulations went into effect in 2001, they made little difference in the oversight of the dietary supplement industry.

There are three claims that can be used on food and dietary supplement labels: health, structure/function, and nutrient claims. Nearly all detox products fall into the FDA category "Structure or Function of the

Body." Claims made about products in this type require no FDA approval (unlike those touting disease treatment or prevention) ("The claims game: The consumer loses" 2001: 5). Rather, manufacturers are responsible for ensuring the accuracy and truthfulness of their stated claims (*Claims That Can Be Made for Conventional Foods and Dietary Supplements* 2001).

This FDA loophole has raised significant concerns within the medical community, especially as research reveals disappointing results with these products. For example, a recent report on thirty of the most popularly used vitamin and mineral supplements, from beta carotene to zinc, shows that the scientific community endorses the use of only one-third of them (viz., beta carotene, calcium, coenzyme Q-10, folic acid, multivitamins, saw palmetto, St. John's wort, vitamin C, vitamin E, and zinc). The other twenty are not recommended and indeed four may be harmful to one's health (viz., chaparral, DHEA, ephedra, and sassafras, which is banned by the FDA yet still sold) ("Dietary supplements" 1998).

Whenever the varied detox products list ingredients (they are not required to), they typically include Vitamin B, creatine, glucose, fructose, dextrose, carbohydrates, citric acids, and various natural herbs, such as red clover, peppermint, dandelion, alfalfa, goldenseal, chamomile, burdock, slippery elm, and rosehips. Diuretics, such as furosemide or uva ursis, do not appear among the listed ingredients. Although these ingredients are not harmful, positive effects from them currently are dubious.

A more recent publication examined the use of creatine, which is commonly listed in detox products. A supplement designed to improve athletic performance by improving anaerobic activities, creatine is an amino acid that, unlike others, is not incorporated into protein but plays a role in energy production. Reported side effects of creatine include diarrhea, dizziness, and cramping; long-term effects are unknown. As is the case with a number of supplements, since there is no governmental regulation, there is no guarantee that one is actually getting creatine or how much or how little appears in any dietary supplement ("Creatine: Behind the hype" 2002: 6).

Perhaps one of the most commonly used herbal detox products is goldenseal, a perennial yellow flower related to the buttercup. A unique development in the study of this flower is that its active ingredients have been identified—hydrastine and berberine, the latter of which is known to work against diarrhea. Beyond this use, at this time there is no known scientific evidence supporting its ability to do anything, much less supporting the fantastic claims made about its detoxing abilities.

The medical community typically does not prescribe goldenseal because it is unpredictable and has potential side effects (e.g., stomach problems, nervousness, depression, respiratory failure).[6] Some within the medical community caution against using any goldenseal because of the unknown quantity of it as sold in its various and unregulated forms. Beyond health benefits allegedly connected with goldenseal, claims continue to be prop-agated that it has the ability to flush out such drugs as marijuana, cocaine, and heroin and thus prevent their detection in urinalyses. But, the med-ical evidence (as opposed to folk or anecdotal evidence) does not support such claims. Much of goldenseal's widespread use and marketing success for flushing purposes is due to little more than folklore; scientific research indicates that goldenseal does not work as a method of masking or elim-inating drugs from one's system (Nebelkopf 1987: 704). And, as is typi-cal of the way humans are driven to consume and profit, in the rush to harvest, goldenseal, in the United States, is now listed as an endangered species ("Goldenseal: Flower power" 1999: 7). But, goldenseal is child's play compared to the products currently marketed within the detox in-dustry. The various detox ingestible items with slick packaging and fan-tastic claims have surpassed natural herbs as detoxing aids.

Among the various diets and "wash-out" regimens, none has been sci-entifically validated. A recent medical-school publication warned against quackery in the United States, which costs consumers several billion dol-lars annually. The advice offered in that publication is that whenever products carry such claims as "cleanse and purify your body" or "rid you of toxins," they should be viewed with considerable skepticism ("If it ducks like a quack" 1999: 6). Nonetheless, for desperate and gullible job applicants or employees, such products and methods, especially given the level of advertising and hype, must seem to them the perfect solution. De-spite accolades from various satisfied customers, these products and tech-niques "have no good scientific foundation and have been found to be un-reliable" (Gieringer 1992: 4). Indeed, among the many individuals inter-viewed for this research was a chemist employed with a company that manufactures detoxification and "wash-out" products as well as items unrelated to the detox industry. He and a couple of other manufacturing employees expressed some misgivings about the efficacy of their products.

A: I'll deny this if you claim I said it, but I wonder why this stuff works this way. As a scientist this doesn't make sense. Someone in the company asked me how these things work and I don't know.

So, I'm going to do some research and help this person understand and will help you understand. [I know someone who]
smokes, so getting a sample should be easy. The vice-president
and I were talking the other day, and he said, "You know, it's
amazing. I don't know how it works." And our company has a
double-the-money-back guarantee for dissatisfied customers and
the vice-president said that we have a 1 to 2 percent return rate. I
frankly have my doubts about this product, but when I see these
kinds of success rates, I begin thinking that there must be something to it.

(Private Interview, March 1999)

He asked that I give him ample time to conduct his research. A few
months later, I talked with him again. He reported the following:

A: [This company] hired me only to do research on how their products work. I suggested that before they spend a lot of their money,
I should look at the literature. I used a web search engine and
looked at Med Line, Drugs, Drug Testing, one of those, and discovered two well-researched, sound, scientific publications saying
that the products have a diuretic effect.
Q: And have you reported this to your superiors?
A: Yes, and they gave no reaction to the news. I think they probably
knew it but chose to deny it. They believe in their products.

(Private Interview, August 1999)

His explanation is that the products work solely by causing frequent urination. A diuretic combined with product instructions to drink large
quantities of water will indeed flush one's system and may well explain
the absence or undetectable traces of drug metabolites in urine assays.
But, taking a diuretic or simply drinking volumes of water is a far less expensive method than using these flush products.

Ongoing Predation

Dietary and herbal supplements have been a part of holistic health and
wellness for centuries. In some parts of the world, Asia in particular, ginseng and other natural herbs are widely used and endorsed. Anecdotal

and experiential evidence abounds as to their health effects. Folk medicines are strongly defended by users who often have first-hand knowledge
of their efficacy. Although important evidence in its own right, first-hand
and anecdotal indications are uniquely different defenses of supplements
than medical knowledge. Despite the medical field's problems, its entrenchment in profit-maximization efforts, and its imperialist marketing
of pharmaceuticals, medical knowledge depends on a far longer tradition
of controlled research than experiential or anecdotal knowledge. When
these products are studied according to the scientific method (and especially experimental designs), health benefits from dietary and herbal supplements do not stand up very well. In other words, to date there is little
medical-scientific evidence supporting their efficacy, despite claims to the
contrary by holistic health advocates.

With any dietary or herbal supplement, a significant problem for consumers is that they have no way of learning a product's exact contents.
For example, a study of St. John's wort, a popular herbal antidepressant,
found that some brands sold had only 20 percent of potency listed, others had only 50 to 90 percent, and still others were 30 to 40 percent more
potent than labeled ("Wellness facts" 1998: 1). More recently, supplements sold as ginseng were found to contain no ginseng whatsoever. In all
fairness, some supplements are not yet well understood by the scientific
community while research on others continues to show that they are in-
effective for the purposes claimed by manufacturers and retailers.

Conclusion

Detox products, like the myriad items discussed above, may well be part
of a growing consortium of predation by companies cashing in during an
historical moment of lax regulation. According to the U.S. General Accounting Office, thirty-one billion dollars were spent on dietary supplements during 1999. The detox business alone is a multi-million-dollar industry within a multi-billion-dollar vitamin and mineral trade. (As noted
in chapter 2, the drug-testing industry also is a multi-billion-dollar enterprise.)

Both the detox and vitamin, mineral, and supplement industries depend, at least in part, on desperate and gullible consumers. In each case,
profits are made as consumers define these products as the panacea for
their chronic problems. They are defined as a quick fix or easy solution

for significant and probably ongoing troubles. Myopic consumers like nothing more than bottled miracles. For the health conscious, the hope is for better and improved health and longevity. For the drug user, the hope is to fool employers long enough to secure or maintain gainful employment.

Detox consumers, like patients visiting their medical doctors, are seeking a way out of their current dilemma. Detox consumers' purchase and use of detox products is as rational as visiting one's doctor for a minor ailment; in each case, for most people, the solution is mysterious. Few patients know very much about bio-medicine; fewer still know much about metabolites, urine testing, and fat-soluble drugs. As a result, in each case, the knowledge possessed within legitimate authority is privileged over lay knowledge. Given the hierarchy of knowledge, patients and consumers probably are acting rationally by seeking the counsel and products of the experts. And in each case, the expert advice and commodity proves effective. But it is equally true that consumers hoping to negate drug testing do not really need the $29.95 Quik Caps, just as patients with minor ailments do not really need the fifty-dollar doctor's office visit. In each instance, time, patience, and common sense probably would have proven just as effective. Results oftentimes stem from the process rather than the product. There is nothing inherent in the purchased commodity that produces the desired result. This is similar to the countless number of individuals who visit their medical doctor for one ailment or another and who, after an exam, are told to, for example, "stay off it," "give it some rest," "take an over-the-counter anti-inflammatory," "stop smoking," or "change diets." None of these treatments and prescriptions are special; each relies on common sense and widely known procedures for achieving desired results. Seeing the doctor and especially paying the fee have nothing to do with the ultimate "cure" or desired outcome. The same is probably the case with detox products used for negating drug tests. Buying a forty-dollar Carbo Drink is unnecessary if casual drug users rely on their own common sense about detoxing.

Rational-choice theory is further relevant to this conundrum. It is applicable to both parties participating in the exchange—the for-profit detox business and the detox consumer/worker. The detox industry in the United States (and elsewhere) operates within the logic of capitalism—a system that rewards cost-cutting, profit-making and false-need-creating practices. This is not to imply that capitalism rewards only unscrupulous business behavior. Completely honest businesses also thrive. But, in some cases, "honesty is discouraged because it contradicts the logic of the enterprise; dishonesty is rewarded because it cuts costs or increases earnings" (Blumberg 1989: 173). Thus the logic of capitalism and the taken-for-granted rules of the market system often reward people for acting in ways that advance their own monetary interests, others be damned. People and businesses behave "rationally and logically in response to the imperatives of a system" (Blumberg 1989: 174). It is this very system in this particular space and time that has given rise to drug testing as policy, a for-profit drug-testing industry, and its for-profit antithesis.

If industry in the United States, supported by government policy, suddenly saw a need for genetic testing of applicants (which is not an impossibility), then profit-maximizing companies would start cranking out testing mechanisms and devices. The logic of the system would produce nothing less. Or if industry, with support from government policy, believed that workers consuming diets high in fat were less productive than workers on low-fat diets, the logic of the system would create devices and procedures for testing and weeding out potentially less productive workers. Capitalism again would produce for-profit industries for detecting defective genes or saturated fat. In any case, the economic system responds by manufacturing and marketing commodities to fill both real and false needs. The market also would produce commodities used for duping such tests.

Consumers define commodities in various terms; desperate consumers define commodities of desperation, such as quick-fix detox products for negating drug tests, as an absolute need and are grateful for their availability. Within the context of rational-choice theory, use of the products for subverting drug tests is rational. The products claim all sorts of benefits (including a double-the-money-back guarantee) and consumers have few alternative actions available for consideration. Choosing *for* the detox product to solve their immediate problems is as rational as choosing to see a doctor for a minor ailment. The benefits of doing so far surpass any negative consequences; alternative choices for the decision maker will not produce the desired result.

According to rational-choice theory, decisions theoretically include assessment of the rewards and risks associated with a given decision problem. Likewise, alternative actions are assessed similarly. Rational decisions are made on the basis of an evaluation of the various rewards and risks of each choice available. There are few risks associated with using detox products; there is little likelihood of one being detected while using them. For desperate consumers, using the products yields only benefits. Alternative decisions are few in number and, as a result, require little rational contemplation when the consumer is choosing. For example, the single most important alternative is to simply stop using drugs several weeks prior to looking for work and submitting to drug testing. Most drug-using workers and job seekers, like nonusing workers and job seekers, are hedonistic. As a result, the alternative of abstinence denies them the pleasures of social drug use and becomes an undue sacrifice. If one chooses against desisting for a time prior to drug testing, there is another alternative: detoxing without a detox product by using those commonly recognized procedures of flushing—eating fruits and vegetables, exercising, and taking vitamin supplements. But, again, workers interviewed for this study have greater faith in the marvels of detox products than these other do-it-yourself methods. As a result, workers define their purchase and use of detox products as more rational and reliable than the use of other commonsense methods and procedures.

Rational-choice theory also highlights the importance of making informed decisions, meaning that decision makers should possess all the information necessary for making logical and rational choices. Most consumers (at least those interviewed for this study) possess little knowledge about their own bodies, the biological processes of expelling various toxins through metabolites, or the hocus-pocus of detox products used for negating drug tests. As a result, in the main, decisions are made with less than complete information. Thus, according to theoretical explications of rational-choice theory, decisions, in this case, may be less than rational. As a result, workers/consumers are making situationally bounded decisions, that is, they are acting with "limited rationality." In such cases, individuals allegedly make a few simple and concrete examinations of their opportunities and make decisions that can be far short of optimal. The fact that individuals do not always make the most rational decisions, that they may pay undue attention to less important information, and that they employ shortcuts while processing information is relevant to understanding empirical decision making and its divergence from theoretical models of rational choice (see, e.g., Piquero and Tibbetts 2002; Tunnell 2002). This procedure certainly characterizes those consumers of detox products who use them for the sole purpose of negating drug testing.

4

Drug Testing as
Social Monitoring and Control

Drug testing, the social monitoring of job applicants and workers, is a component of general and dynamic processes of social control (e.g., Borg and Arnold 1997; Garland 2001; Gilliom 1994, 2001). Drug testing represents a fundamental shift in workplace employer-employee relations and is one of many of an increasing number of intrusions into workers' privacy (Wagner 1987).

Workers in the contemporary United States are subject to various methods of surveillance and resulting control. From eavesdropping on employees' telephone conversations and monitoring Internet use to intercepting e-mail correspondence, employers are whittling away at workers' previously taken-for-granted privacy. For example, employees have not always worked in situations where employers eavesdropped. Only in recent years have consumers, while on the telephone with one business or another, heard the recorded message, "This conversation may be recorded for quality control purposes." Previous generations of workers were subject, for example, to having lunch boxes and purses searched or were forced to punch time cards. Control methods today, however, are vastly different.

These modifications in some respects reflect changing technologies that are used in the workplace and that offer employers heretofore unknown surveillance modes and strategies. In other words, they may be technologically determined modes of control. They also are part of larger social and punitive changes in people's everyday lives and particularly in the workplace. There workers' autonomy and future are threatened. For example, during the data collection for this research, one particular company's human resource officer, who oversees workplace drug testing, was interviewed. Based on his initiative, the company recently had implemented a new program for responding to workers' absences from work.

In the past, workers' absences were overlooked as long as they produced medical verification (viz., a note from their doctor). Believing that workers were abusing the privilege of being ill and seeking medical treatment, the company initiated a new "No Fault Plan" whereby absences, regardless of the type, are now regarded as unexcused. Those abusing the system by missing a fixed number of days from work now find their employment, health, and livelihood in jeopardy. This policy, especially given the company's drug-testing strategy, is in some respects contradictory. In the case of sick leave, the company's new policy actually surveils workers less than before. Absences are neither questioned nor verified. The reason for missing work is irrelevant and is unmonitored. Ironically the company's new sick leave policy enables far greater control over workers. They are now simply threatened with termination for missing work regardless of the reason. Their missing work is recorded, not investigated. Workers know the consequences and are reluctant to miss work for any reason. Thus, they are controlled in ways unknown before.

Beyond lengthy background investigations, several rounds of interviews, and polygraph, integrity, physical, and psychological screening, drug testing as a condition of employment has quickly become a primary technique for distinguishing the reputable from the disreputable. As a means of differentiating, it is considerably less expensive than background, physical, or psychological investigations. It also, unlike polygraph exams, is admissible in court. Given drug testing's widespread acceptance, it has become standard operating procedure within innumerable private and public work settings. Employees testing positive are responded to in various ways by their employers. For example, companies react by issuing warnings or suspending employees, by forcing them into drug rehabilitation, or by simply and immediately terminating their employment. Coerced rehabilitation is a questionable policy, especially for those individuals most commonly detected for drug use—marijuana smokers. Termination, as a corporate response, typically occurs only after corroborating tests such as the GC/MS have been performed. In most cases, applicants who test positive are not hired and oftentimes are prohibited from re-applying for a fixed period of time (usually six to twelve months). In some cases, applicants are not allowed to apply for work with that company again.

Drug testing, as it currently functions, is not without problems and limitations. For example, urinalyses results consistently show greater drug use than that reported by subjects—raising doubts about both the reliability of self-reported drug-using data and the realities of false-positive test results. Furthermore, frequently abused drugs such as cocaine and some opiates generally are not detectable by urinalysis after forty-eight hours from ingestion, leaving these more serious drugs of abuse mainly undiscovered by current testing procedures. As a result, new and more precise drug-testing methods, especially hair analyses, are currently propagated as necessary.

The presence of drugs in hair samples is detected by using RIA and ultrasensitive GC/MS procedures. Hair follicles preserve drug metabolites for a much longer time than does urine. Cocaine, which metabolizes quickly, is detected much more easily and for a much longer period of time in hair than in urine. To date, research findings on detecting marijuana metabolites in hair with reliable degrees of specificity are mixed. Although problems remain with hair testing (e.g., subjects with very short hair, costs versus benefits), its use, in all likelihood, will increase (see, e.g., Mieczkowski 1997).

Private companies specializing in testing body hair for drug metabolites have increased in number across recent years. The emergence of this facet of the drug-testing industry was encouraged after a decade of research funded largely by the National Institute of Justice, the United States Navy, and the American Society for Industrial Security. The agencies concluded that hair-follicle analysis is necessary for establishing a zero-tolerance workplace.

A recent CBS investigative report indicated considerable variance in the ability to detect drug metabolites in hair. With the exception of Psychemedics Corporation of Cambridge, Massachusetts, which was vindicated during the program for its ability to correctly identify every positive and negative sample, other companies were unable to consistently detect and identify contaminated samples. According to Psychemedics Corporation, it currently performs hair analysis for over sixteen hundred corporations, law enforcement agencies, banks, parole offices, schools, and universities. The company claims that it not only can detect the presence of a drug in a hair sample but also can provide accurate information on the quantity and history of drug use. Furthermore, according to company claims, its procedures can detect the presence of drug use as many as ninety days prior to sample collection and testing. Such drug-testing procedures may be the wave of the future, especially if employers are determined, convinced, and coerced to hire and retain exceptionally drug-free employees.

Given the increasing use of various detox products and techniques used to produce false-negative test results, corporate devices to counter these duping initiatives recently have emerged. For example, BioScan Screening System's Intect 6 is a device marketed as a convenient, easy-to-use dipstick that identifies substances commonly used to interfere with urinalysis screening. The Intect 6 is simply dipped into the urine sample, and colors on the reagent strip correspond with a color-coded chart. The device yields nearly immediate results so that, if necessary, a second sample can be collected from the donor while she/he is on the premises. According to company literature, Intect 6 detects excessive fluid consumption, as well as the products Klear, UrinAid, Instant Clean, and do-it-yourself subversion additives such as bleach, vinegar, eyewash products, sodium bicarbonate, drain cleaners, soft drinks, and hydrogen peroxide. It makes no claims about its ability to detect flushing and masking detox products. Beyond its detection advantages, the product is inexpensive—only one dollar for twenty-five strips. Thus, in efforts at extending social control and individuals' attempts at subverting it, we witness ongoing point-counterpoint maneuvers as each party jockeys for advantage.

These subversion-neutralizing products are but a minor part of the overall control industry (of which the crime-industrial complex is a part). For a perusal of some scary advertisements for other surveillance and control products, pick up a recent copy of *Corrections Today*. Or await the arrival of (or if you can't wait, order) the latest product catalog published by SIRCHIE Fingerprint Laboratories of Youngsville, North Carolina. Although fingerprinting items comprise the bulk of the advertised products, SIRCHIE offers forensic equipment, riot gear, and an on-site drug-testing system called NARK Presumptive Drug Test Kit. These and other products of social control are now part of a multi-billion-dollar annual business of surveilling, neutralizing, controlling, and containing large numbers of individuals defined as undesirables by both public and private entities (see, e.g., Christie 1994; Tunnell 1992b).

Expanding Social Control

Social control contains both a normative system of values and formal and informal mechanisms for responding to deviance from normative conduct. Formal social control exists in the legitimate authority of the law, in the criminal justice system, and with employers, among others. Informal

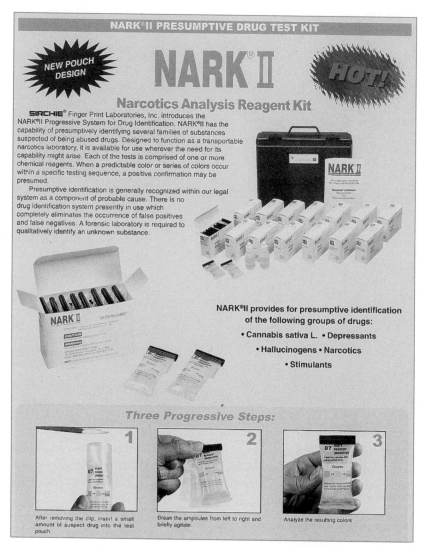

IRCHIE NARKII Presumptive Drug Test Kit. *Courtesy of SIRCHIE.*

social control is located in the family, among primary group members, neighborhoods and elsewhere when relations typically (but not solely) are intimate and personal. Social control theories tend to treat these two types of control as inversely related so that when informal control measures are lacking, formal control initiatives increase. Likewise, informal control increases during lapses in formal control (see, e.g., Akers 1994: chapter 2).

The theoretical work of Donald Black seems pertinent to this phenomenon of increasing social control generally and increasing formal control specifically in the workplace. Extrapolating from his thesis, one can conclude that drug testing is far likelier within large, heterogeneous organizations characterized by distant social relations and with employees who possess either suspicious or disreputable social status (Black 1984: volume 1). In these cases, informal social controls typically are weak and those in possession of formal control measures suspect their subordinates. Testing suspicious populations for drug use is another means by which reputation can be verified. Drug testing as social monitoring or control is a means by which deviance or disreputability is easily defined—indeed, by a single measure—and responded to.

The means by which individuals within smaller organizations are evaluated, monitored, and controlled are highly different. Within small, intimate groups, social monitoring largely occurs informally as the social bond and tight relations limit deviance and react accordingly to it. Yet within most contemporary working relations, intimacy rarely exists and informal control measures are replaced by impersonal, rationalized, hierarchical, bureaucratized systems that are applicable to every office and office holder.[1]

This tendency toward rationalization of institutions of both the private and public sectors is a feature of contemporary capitalism. Rationalization is a means-end calculation within modern organizations as life becomes increasingly dominated by formal policies and procedures and with rules based on rational-legal authority (Weber 1922/1978). "The mark of formal social monitoring, or surveillance, is its organization. Surveillance impersonally and deliberately provides information that is standardized and precise" (Borg and Arnold 1997: 444). Such qualities are central to the concept of rationalization.

Black's thesis has been supported by recent research that indicates that as organizational relations become more distant, culturally more diverse, and composed of individuals with some reputation for deviance (or at least under suspicion), drug testing becomes much more likely. "Drug testing, an example of formal monitoring, most often emerges in a context marked by relational distance and low normative respectability"—a far different scenario than that found within intimate, personal settings (Borg and Arnold 1997: 456).

Lyon (1994) describes the unprecedented extent to which people in contemporary societies find themselves under surveillance while engaged in their everyday routines. But, for Lyon, surveillance is not simply and unambiguously only positive or only negative. It can be and often is both. This certainly seems the case with drug testing for employment. Consider the varied responses to workplace drug testing. Civil libertarians, constitutional scholars, and a whole host of working men and women, for example, may define workplace drug testing as the grossest form of privacy invasion; they may also define it as personally and publicly demeaning, as they are required to urinate on demand in the presence of a monitor. Yet others, including one's employers and coworkers, may define it as a positive and necessary social development as they believe that testing contributes to a drug-free, safer, and more productive workplace. Some employers may define testing as little more than a governmental mandate while others may consider it a means of reducing personnel costs and hence increasing profits. Consumers may define drug testing of, say, airline pilots as a perfectly reasonable public policy but may question the necessity of testing every person who applies for clerical work with their local Walmart. Some view this new form of surveillance as representing a "disciplinary practice which ensure[s] that life continues in a regularized, patterned way" (Foucault 1979: 7) while others recognize a distinction between surveillance as data collection (for basic research, for example) and that used to monitor, oversee, and ultimately discipline entire classes of people.

For others, drug testing is yet another procedure for determining a person's reputability. Given that the United States and other industrial and postindustrial societies are largely composed of throngs of strangers living within a Durkheimian organic (dis)order, such measures of establishing reputation aid employers, for example, in delineating those strangers (whether applicant or employee) who use various drugs from those who do not. Drug testing, as surveillance, is a relatively easy solution for employers who have few methods available for distinguishing reputable from disreputable individuals (as defined solely by procedures that detect drug use). Drug screening as surveillance, which is vastly different from psychological testing, yields concrete and precise bio-chemical data. That information alone indicates something about one's reputation and provides the means by which strangers can at least minimally evaluate and later trust or distrust strangers. Complex societies have always produced and valued various methods for establishing and maintaining reputations—both the good and the bad. This is accomplished in part by formally recognizing and then relying on individuals' credentials and the results of various ordeals (i.e., rituals for determining the truth, such as polygraph, psychological, integrity, and drug testing) (Nock 1993: 3).

In societies filled with strangers, and stranger-to-stranger surveillance, privacy itself becomes a highly valued privilege. For example, the horrors resulting from an entirely public life were detailed when George Orwell's protagonists Winston and Julia established a private apartment for romantic encounters that presumably was away from the ever-watchful gaze of Big Brother (Orwell 1949). Within heterogeneous, organic societies, as relationships continue to be characterized as superficial, anomic, and distrustful, privacy becomes highly important, especially to those fortunate enough to possess it or to those desperate enough to demand it, such as Orwell's characters. Since strangers, by definition, have no reputation or credentials, ordeals and surveillance are used to determine trustworthiness or reputability. It is, in part, the inability to intimately know about others and their personal lives that contributes to the increasing practice of spying on others and placing them under surveillance. "Privacy is one consequence, or cost, of growing numbers of strangers. Surveillance is one consequence, or cost, of privacy" (Nock 1993: 11). In advanced societies privacy and surveillance are counterrelated symmetrical events. Surveillance, as a result, remains ambiguous as it is regarded as both a positive and negative feature of complex, postmodern, organic societies.

Drug testing, as an ordeal, is a highly ritualistic process for determining reputability. Less developed cultures have relied on various rituals such as mystical signs, gods, physical tests of endurance, and abilities to tolerate pain for determining reputability. Rather than mysticism, developed societies rely on science to yield a verdict about reputation, as is the case with the ritualized ordeal of drug testing. Modern ordeals relying generally on science are most common in "larger communities, those with intermediate or high political integration, high degrees of economic complexity, and more elaborate forms of jurisdictional hierarchy" (Nock 1993: 83).

Various ordeals have been implemented across this century to uncover deception or to establish reputation. For example, the lie detector or polygraph test was used by private employers for years, primarily for screening preemployment applicants. In 1987, Congress passed the Polygraph Protection Act, which prohibited the use of polygraph exams as a condition of employment and as a random workplace surveillance tactic. During the last year polygraph exams were used in employment situations, about two million tests were performed by private employers (Nock 1993: 90). Since then, other measures of reputability have emerged.

Given the legal prohibition of polygraph exams, employers have turned increasingly to integrity testing (aka honesty testing). Today, over six thousand employers currently use such measures. Several million integrity tests are performed annually, primarily as part of preemployment application processes (Nock 1993: 92). As with polygraph and drug screening, integrity testing is most commonly applied to individuals who possess few credentials and who, as strangers, possess reputations that are not so easily discernible. As is the case with polygraph and drug screening, integrity testing is used primarily on applicants for lower-status and safety-sensitive jobs and rarely on applicants for managerial positions or among those holding reputable credentials. Thus, in all cases, class, status, and hierarchical location are inversely related to those subject to highly ritualized tests for establishing reputation. Such exams are the final ordeal in a series to which employees or prospective employees are subjected. As discussed earlier in relation to detox products, integrity tests are proprietary and researchers, to date, have had little success in gaining access to them or to information about the validity of their procedures. Although bold claims are made about their efficacy within the industrial psychology community, little independently verified evidence about their alleged marvels exists. Just as with drug screening and detoxing, integrity testing is problematic and its use appeals as much to the appearance of science and to informed decisions as to science itself (see, e.g., Nock 1993).

In the main, these rituals are status-degradation ceremonies, a descriptive and analytical concept within social psychology and dramaturgy. Status-degradation ceremonies are highly ritualized processes. In fact, as Durkheim might argue, it is the rituals themselves that give particular meanings to ceremonies. Airline passengers increasingly are subject to highly routinized, indeed ritualistic procedures as they are searched, questioned, and scanned. In this situation, passengers can hardly help but feel uncomfortable and as if they are suspects. The screening and questioning process oftentimes makes passengers feel as if they are something less than what they were only minutes earlier (traveling consumers). Relatedly, to workers (and, increasingly, students), pissing on demand also is a highly ritualized and humiliating ceremony. It becomes ritualistic as company drug-testing procedures are articulated in testing policies. Drug-testing operatives are instructed to follow carefully calculated and precise steps when collecting, securing, and analyzing urine samples. The steps ideally are the same for each subject; the ritual of urine testing becomes highly routinized. When one is required to piss on demand, it undoubtedly is a humiliating experience. Company (or school) urine-collection monitors instruct each subject to wash her hands and take a urine specimen cup into a public restroom stall. In most cases, the monitor is instructed to visually observe the subject while she urinates into the cup. In some cases monitors are instructed to wait outside the bathroom stall and listen for the telltale sounds. Most individuals subject to pissing on demand define the process as embarrassing. Lindsay Earls of Tecumseh, Oklahoma, reported feeling "humiliated."

Status-degradation ceremonies are indeed ceremonial or ritualistic processes of dishonoring one's social standing within one's community. Status degradation nearly always occurs as the less powerful are subject to the machinations of the more powerful. Airport personnel are security operatives exercising their power over travelers who experience, if only temporarily, the detrimental effects of status degradation. Police, judges, and prosecutors, representing the state's force, law, and administration, have immense power to adversely affect one's reputation and status. Drug-testing operatives likewise enjoy a power as they are charged with imposing specific ceremonies on others who are humiliated and thus experience the devaluing of their social location.

Discipline and Social Control

Staples, whose focus is on a far-ranging culture of surveillance, describes "meticulous rituals of power," or "micro techniques of discipline and social control," that are made possible by new technologies and procedures or innovative uses of tried and true methods and technologies. These micro techniques and new technologies and procedures are "knowledge gathering" devices and methods that rely on "surveillance, information, and evidence collection and analysis" (Staples 1997: 3). Staples refers to the methods and procedures as meticulous because "they are small procedures and techniques that are precisely and thoroughly exercised." He refers to them as ritualistic because "they are faithfully repeated and are often quickly accepted and routinely practiced with little question." Power is important to these methods and techniques because "they are intended to discipline people into acting in ways that others have deemed to be lawful or have defined as appropriate or simply normal" (Staples 1997: 3). The micro techniques, meticulously and ritualistically performed, are part of macro disciplinary strategies. They possess qualities that are distinctly new, and as some have argued, postmodern in form and process.

According to Foucault (1979), the modern era gave rise to various methods and procedures intended to shape both body and mind. This uniquely modern style of social and political stricture Foucault labeled "disciplinary power," a type of power that is processual in form yet distinct from power in the traditional sociological sense of the word (i.e, something held over and used to control others). Disciplinary, unlike traditional Weberian, conceptualizations of power (i.e., *Macht*, see, e.g., Walliman et al. 1980) is bidirectional. In other words, it does not simply proceed from the top in a downward direction or from the powerful to the less powerful. Rather, it is fluid and enmeshed in social relations to the extent that it dynamically circulates throughout the social body.

> So rather than being concentrated in the hands of a few, disciplinary power appears nearly everywhere, dispersed and fragmented. The exercise of disciplinary power is often continuous, automatic, and anonymous (think of the surveillance video camera, for example). It is extensive and thorough, and it is capillary as well, meaning that it extends out to the remotest corners of society. It disciplines individuals efficiently and effectively, with the least amount of physical force, labor power and expense. (Staples 1997: 25)

As for Staples, for Foucault knowledge is essential to the circulation of disciplinary power, but knowledge and power are not synonymous; rather, each presupposes the other. Drug testing as disciplinary power requires no physical force. The labor exerted for collecting and analyzing samples is minimal. With the increased use of on-site testing procedures, costs, according to industry spokespersons anyway, are negligible.[2] Drug testing as disciplinary power is capillary and has spread everywhere, from the business centers of New York to the hills of Los Angeles, making stops and taking hold along the way in such locales as the coal fields of Tire Hill, Pennsylvania, the lumber mills of Job, West Virginia, the offices of Bland, Missouri, the construction sites of Cement, Oklahoma, and (perhaps the place with the most ironic name for the dichotomies of positive-negative or reputable-disreputable) Truth or Consequences, New Mexico, and a host of other unknown hamlets where workers are simply trying to earn a living, raise their families, and live their lives. Workers everywhere are now subject to this new, decentralized form of disciplinary power.

Drug testing in the workplace (or other places among the remotest corners of society) is an exercise of disciplinary power (or a meticulous ritual of power) that relies on biological and physiological knowledge to obtain biological knowledge. In other words, drug testing uses knowledge of the body to extract information about the body, which is then used to assess and, if need be, discipline the body (and in some cases mind, spirit, and livelihood).

Disciplinary power is not solely repressive. It also is treated by Foucault as productive (which is similar to Lyon's position that surveillance is not unambiguously positive or negative; it can be and often is both). For example, if disciplinary power were only repressive, it probably would be met with various degrees of resistance and open defiance, perhaps to the point that it would, by force or coercion, undergo fundamental alteration. But, the ambiguous character of disciplinary power highlights its positive functions or its productivity. The processes of disciplinary power are corrective; the goals are to modify behavior and to reward conformity—not an inherently negative feature for any society. For example, the disciplinary power of drug testing in the workplace is often viewed by workers as positive and as a process that rewards their abstinence while also keeping them safe from potential drug-using coworkers who may pose a host of problems for them during their working hours. Their hope is that others will conform to the drug-free workplace policies and the social expectations and protocol of securing work and maintaining a job. Although civil libertarians may strongly disagree and vilify these workers as subjects of cultural hegemony (or false consciousness), we cannot summarily dismiss the positive functions that they identify in drug testing.

Disciplinary power is further manifested through particular procedures, such as "the examination," a highly ritualized process whereby knowledge is gathered about individuals' lives. The process by which the examination and knowledge gathering serve the dominant order includes two important elements—hierarchical observation and normalizing judgments. Hierarchical observation is a process whereby individuals are surveilled. Yet those doing the watching are also watched by others within the hierarchy. Just as workers' behaviors are observed by their superiors, the latters' supervision is often evaluated by the former. This is further indication that disciplinary power is not concentrated in the hands of a few powerful interests but appears nearly everywhere, decentralized, dispersed, fluid, and fragmented. The second element, normalizing judgments, means measuring individuals and their activities or lifestyles against an articulated standard or ideal type. Individuals, their work behavior, politics, lifestyle—you name it—are judged along a continuum of good or bad; acceptable or unacceptable; reputable or disreputable. In the case of drug testing as observation and normalizing judgment, the continuum is collapsed into a dichotomy of drug user and nonuser, which is dependent on another dichotomy of a positive and a negative test result. With drug testing using urinalyses, the routinized procedures are to measure a sample against a calibrator containing a fixed quantity of the drug for which the sample is tested. Observations are made, judgments rendered, and discipline exercised. Foucault's (1979: 136) position is that these procedures are used to convert individuals into "docile bodies" that, by the very exercise of disciplinary power, are manipulated into an ameliorated state. A body is docile when it may be "subjected, used, transformed and improved."

The modern era witnessed a different treatment of the body than occurred in earlier times. For example, the scale of control of the body shifted from an en masse treatment of hordes of people to an individual-based subtle coercion, or an "infinitesimal power over the active body." Not only did the scale of control shift from behavior to economy (viz., efficiency of movement), but it also shifted in its modality; control became an "uninterrupted, constant coercion" (Foucault 1979: 137) rather than an episodic form that was easily forgettable once encountered and with the ensuing passage of time. These new and highly efficient methods, for Foucault, are disciplines that become general formulas for domination, manipulated and applied to specific social needs for producing docile bodies. As a form of discipline, drug testing is designed to neutralize inconveniences to capital and organizational discipline by manipulating and dominating workers in the remotest corners of productivity.

Other technologies are used to convert active, free-spirited, and independent humans into docile bodies. Consider contemporary home-incarceration techniques, for example, which include such newly emerging technologies as cameras located in subjects' dwellings rather than ankle-fitting electronic monitoring devices. With this form of surveillance, a single, constantly staring camera in one's home exemplifies disciplinary power. Although not as invasive in that it does not also broadcast into the home, it is reminiscent of Orwell's (1949: 6) "telescreen" of the future. The telescreen was always on yet the observed were never certain if they were actually being watched at any given moment. Although the subjects of Orwell's totalitarian society realized that not everyone could be observed at once, they also knew that the authorities could plug into any one camera at any minute. As a result, they behaved as if always under observation. Such postmodern disciplinary technologies are increasingly useful in deriving information from peoples about their activities and their bodies (Staples 1997: 92).

> Once put in place, these new technologies reduce the need to trust offenders to "mend their ways" or for suspects to "speak the truth" as in confessing to the use of drugs, to being at the scene of a crime, or even to having "deviant desires." Rather, it is individuals' objectified bodies that will "tell us what we need to know" and "who they really are" as in such categories as "known drug user," "sexual predator," or someone with a "personality disorder." In other words, it is no longer considered effective or efficient to simply gaze at the body—or to train it in hopes of rendering it docile—rather, we must surveil its inner evidence and secrets. (Staples 1997: 93)

This new form of surveillance is referred to as a "pornography of the self" because it is an obscene gaze that attempts to lay bare an individual's "true" identity.

The Panopticon, originated by British philosopher and penologist Jeremy Bentham, was first applied to individuals confined to prisons. The Panopticon design situated a central tower (which was known as the inspector's lodge) in the middle of a circular building surrounded by prison cells that were back-lit. As a result, from the central tower, prisoners, in their cells, could be constantly watched. The tower, however, had designed into it a system of blinds that precluded prisoners from knowing if they actually were being watched. As a result, they had to behave at all times as if they were under scrutiny. Prisoners internalized what Foucault referred to as "the gaze" of their captors. Power and control operated unabated regardless of whether the tower was occupied or empty. As a form of hypersurveillance, the major effect of the Panopticon was to "induce in the inmate a state of conscious and permanent visibility that assure[d] the automatic functioning of power" (Foucault 1979: 201). The result was that once-undisciplined prisoners became converted into docile bodies due to the constant, ever-present, and conspicuous gaze, as was the case with Orwell's characters.

Although never implemented in its pure form, many of the Panopticon's methods and principles have been adapted by prisons, factories, offices, schools, shopping centers, and inner-city blocks (e.g., Foucault 1979: part 3; Staples 1997: 27–29). These "governmentalities" (to use Foucault's term), or the techniques and processes by which control is exercised over others, include not only the state but also interests and organizations unrelated to it. The result, carried to its extreme, is a self-governmentality or individual self-control. Consider the future, as described by Orwell's hellish vision of fascistic surveillance. Or consider Bentham's hope that the very thought of deviance, or in Orwellian terms, "crimethink" (i.e., deviant thoughts), would become increasingly difficult to entertain. Consider, too, the application of Weber's rationalization and Bentham's Panopticon to changes in the workplace during the twentieth century. The development and application of scientific management resulted in the economy of movement, the routinization and streamlining of work, all while workers became increasingly subject to the gaze of supervision and accountability (Taylor 1911/1982; Braverman 1974).

The random gaze of the Panopticon prison, the home-incarceration camera, video monitors in the workplace, the interception of employees' e-mail correspondence, and drug-testing devices and procedures lead to docility and, in the main, ultimately self-censorship and -control, or obedience. Consider the situation in Washington, D.C., which is now regarded as the video surveillance capital of the United States. It is the most watched city in the nation. Video cameras, monitoring nearly all monuments, plazas, train stations, and public buildings, feed into one centralized video command center located on the 5th floor of the Metropolitan Police Headquarters. According to the authorities, video surveillance is necessary to monitor "traffic flow." A seven-million-dollar project, it has been met with mixed reviews. One passerby claimed that "you feel more safe," while others lament that "just because you have a legal right to do something doesn't mean it's the right thing to do." Plans are underway to expand surveillance into suburbs and possibly into public schools (*All Things Considered* 2002). Evidently, there are traffic flow problems in schools as well.

Foucault's analysis is that with the extension of science to the hierarchical exercise of power on bodies through uniform ritualistic examinations, the end result is self-control and docility—or, in other words, well-behaved people. First concerned with the prison, asylum, and military, Foucault foresaw that these meticulous methods would be ultimately reproduced and transformed into other arenas. Thus, the micro disciplinary techniques of specific institutions are reproduced and extended outward, merging with the needs of other institutions and public places and resulting in a macro web of controlling methods and greater social containment (Foucault 1979; Staples 1997).

Disciplinary power is fluid and makes its way into unforeseen areas, which results in new controls as part of the public's everyday lived experiences. These meticulous rituals of power form a particular order that seemingly has no one central authority directing or overseeing it but that subjects nearly everyone to its consistent gaze and inconsistent whims; its primary objective is an increase in orderliness and the control of undesirable populations. As technologies become increasingly sophisticated, so does the exercise of power in its fluidity, rapidity, lightness, inconspicuousness, and subtle coercive abilities. Such disciplinary power, when working most effectively, becomes a part of a culture's hegemony. Absent defiance and resistance at some level, docility or, at the most, personal and individualized resistance (rather than collective) becomes the norm.

Unlike disciplinary power of a few centuries ago, these new forms impose themselves on individuals as they live their everyday public lives; they no longer require an imposition of power on secluded, segregated, institutionalized individuals. And as disciplinary power reaches into the remotest corners of society, it manifests itself in decentralized methods, as is the case with drug testing and urinalyses being conducted on-site by company employees rather than at centralized medical facilities.

Table 4.1 illustrates increased levels of surveillance in the workplace. In each case other than video recording of job performance, surveillance of workers has increased.

Conclusion

Drug testing as social control is questioned less and less often among both lay persons and jurists, especially given the public's initial reactions to screening. Today, it is widely accepted by unions, their members, professional and nonprofessional employees, job applicants, and a host of others. And as discussed earlier, many employees believe it necessary for their

TABLE 4.1
Workplace Monitoring and Surveillance
(By Type, Year, and Percentage of Firms Using These Methods)

Type of Surveillance	Year 1997	Year 1998	Year 1999	Year 2000	Year 2001
Recording & review of voice mail	10.4	11.2	10.6	11.5	11.9
Storage & review of voice mail	5.3	5.3	5.8	6.8	7.8
Storage & review of computer files	13.7	19.6	21.4	30.8	36.1
Storage & review of e-mail messages	14.9	20.2	27.0	38.1	46.5
Monitoring internet connections	N/A	N/A	N/A	54.1	62.8
Video recording of job performance	15.7	15.6	16.1	14.6	15.2
Telephone use (time spent, numbers called)	34.4	40.2	38.6	44.0	43.3
Computer use (time logged on, keystroke counts)	16.1	15.9	15.2	19.4	18.9
Video surveillance for security	33.7	32.7	32.8	35.3	37.7
Total, all forms of electronic monitoring and/or surveillance	63.4	67.1	67.3		
Including internet monitoring, absent prior to 2000				78.4	82.2
Excluding internet monitoring, as in years previous to 2000				73.4	77.1

Source: 2001 American Management Survey. American Management Association, New York.

own workplace safety. Such changes in attitude across a diverse population such as that within the United States is indicative of cultural hegemony as drug testing becomes an unquestioned process and as this latest form of disciplinary power proceeds largely unabated. Yet, as detailed in chapter 3, an industry has emerged in recent years to counter drug-testing policies and procedures. And, with the rise of the industry, defiant workers and prospective employees are seeking ways to neutralize increasing disciplinary power on their lives. Their resistance to drug testing and other forms of control are detailed in chapter 5.

5

The Politics of Resistance

The Only Urine You'll Get From Me Is for a Taste Test
—bumper sticker, March 2003

Social and private life increasingly is subject to public observation and surveillance. Yet, rather than defeatism characterizing social responses to cultural constraints, resistance is afoot. Granted, surveillance is vastly different today than at any time previously, as chapter 4 details. But, that does not necessarily mean the human spirit is unimaginative. It also does not imply that humans everywhere acquiesce. Rather, the age of surveillance generates varied responses, including acquiescence, a resignation to the status quo, the display of cavalier attitudes, satisfied ignorance of the politics at work, and defiance. Resistance and defiance are age-old responses to control efforts. As is shown in this chapter, people in various social locations and occupations are resisting drug testing. The resistance is similar to defiance of other particular features of social life (e.g., labor activism, antiwar initiatives, environmental struggles, conflicts over lifestyle concerns).

Despite drug testing having become an accepted cultural mode for determining reputation, and despite its entrenchment within sophisticated surveillance methods, it nonetheless has been met, on several fronts, with criticism and resistance. Disparate individuals, interest groups, and newly emerging antitesting industries both critique and defy workplace drug-testing policies and procedures. There are a number of commonly levied complaints, including, for example, that drug testing is an invasion of privacy and that results are neither confidential nor reliable. Testing is also criticized and resisted because it is viewed as yet another tactic in the war on drugs—a public policy characterized as flawed, misplaced, expensive, and punitive—as opposed to one committed to public health and welfare (see, e.g., Trebach and Inciardi 1993; cf. Massing 1998). Furthermore, drug testing is criticized for its sheer financial and social costs. It also is appraised as absent fundamental due processes and as an immoral and unethical approach to containing workplace drug use. Also, critics contend that there is little evidence to suggest that drug testing is an effective policy for controlling drug use in the workplace—which is the real issue, or at least the issue publicly propagated by testing advocates. After all, drug testing, as currently implemented, does not reveal current impairment, only past use. Critics continually raise perhaps the most fundamental question of whether a substantial problem, commensurate with such initiatives, exists or has ever existed.

These criticisms have not fallen on deaf ears. Employers have given similar reasons for abandoning or deciding against adopting drug-testing policies. In fact, of those companies that have chosen not to engage in drug-testing procedures, 63 percent claim that their decisions are based on their surmisal that drug testing is inaccurate and 43 percent cite drug testing's inability to differentiate current impairment from previous use (Zeese 1997: 1–34.24). Beyond statements about the inaccuracies and unreliability of testing, 68 percent of employers recently surveyed consider testing an invasion of their employees' privacy. As a result, some have decided against implementing drug-screening policies. Other employers resist using drug testing because of its adverse impacts on employee morale; indeed, 53 percent of those surveyed report such. And last, but certainly not least of importance to employers, are the sheer financial expenditures associated with testing. A positive finding reportedly costs about seven thousand dollars when one takes into account the expense of testing (reportedly $11 million nationally per year), the few positive results, costlier corroborating tests, and MRO consultations.

The financial argument is a particularly salient one. The *Drug Testing Index,* a semiannual survey, shows that positive results continue to decline, with an overall positive rate of 4.7 percent during 1999, down from 4.8 in 1998 (1999). Among federally mandated safety-sensitive positions, positive findings were at 3.2 percent. The positive results for the overall work force continue their steady downward trend, which began in 1988 when testing showed 13.6 percent of results as being positive (*Drug Testing Index* 1999). Such data, especially within transportation—the industry that first adopted broad testing programs—continue to raise critical questions about the cost-effectiveness of these particular public policies since declining positive findings increase the costs of detecting such findings (see, e.g., Zeese 1997: 1–37).

The detox industry, while financially capitalizing on this new form of surveillance into workers' lives, has in the main been relatively quiet about the politics of drug use, drug testing, and testing subterfuge. However, a small minority of manufacturers has entered the political fray by making a modicum of public statements about the war on drugs, drug testing in the workplace, and its impact on civil liberties. For example, Health Tech's literature claims that while it does not advocate illegal drug use while on the job, "what a person does in their own time in the privacy of their home is their business." Health Tech supports workers being evaluated on the basis of job performance rather than private, after-hours leisure activities. The company also interprets the 4th and 5th Amendments to the Constitution as protections against these intrusions into individuals' personal lives. Company literature claims that "drug tests also violate the constitutional guarantee of presumption of innocence, placing the burden of proof on the accused." The claim is made that workers currently are treated as guilty, and the burden of proving otherwise is shifted to them. The company is not far off the mark with this criticism. As described earlier, states' laws have shifted the burden of proof to the accused, in support of companies that implement testing programs. Jeff Nightbyrd, who was among the first to market clean urine and then drug-free powdered urine, also has publicly criticized drug testing. From his website, nodrugwar.com, he admonishes, "Test Your Government. Not Your Urine."

A few detox companies advocate collective action to end, as we now know it, drug testing in the workplace, which is ironic, for such changes in public policy ultimately would threaten the detox industry's production, sales, and profiting. Most detox companies, however, manufacture and market their products without publicly taking positions on or issuing statements about drug use or workplace drug testing.

Resistance among Workers and Detox Consumers

Consumers' general experiences with detox products and the way they discover, acquire, and use them vary. Most individuals interviewed for this research learned about them through word of mouth, purchased them at local health-food or head shops, and followed products' instructions to the letter. In the main, the workers/consumers interviewed for this research were casual marijuana users who were subject to preemployment drug testing. They were drug tested for jobs that were not in transportation or of a safety-sensitive nature and that did not put themselves or others at risk of injury. These consumers intimated to me that, in effect, they attempt to compartmentalize their working from their private lives. They hope to maintain their privacy and private drug use while remaining gainfully employed.

Consumers interviewed for this research used a detox product only once, for the very job that they now hold or the one held previously. As a group, they maintain relatively steady and stable employment with most of them remaining with the same employer for several years. They also tend to maintain relatively stable drug use. Indeed, detox product consumers interviewed for this research use marijuana almost solely. Two participants reportedly have used cocaine, but erratically. They offered a number of reasons as to why they use cocaine irregularly rather than more frequently: its price, its availability, and its short-term and, in some cases, unpleasant effects. As a group, they intimated that they also prefer the effects of marijuana over those of cocaine.

These participants disclosed similar experiences with detox products and marvel at their ability to dupe the tests. Oftentimes referring to their boss, drug-testing operatives, MROs, or whomever, as "the man," they seemingly enjoy duping these individuals and invariably credit their success to detox products. They articulate a faith in the products' magic. Of course, we cannot overlook the possibility that this simply might be a face-saving device. After all, each person interviewed had shelled out thirty or forty dollars for the product. Each passed the test and landed the job. At this point, they probably would feel compromised by admitting skepticism about the very commodity that they believe helped them beat "the man" and in which they are psychologically and monetarily invested.

The following conversation was held with one detox consumer as he explained his experience with the product itself and the drug-testing process. Although tested when applying for a job, today he is self-employed in a major city and his business, in his words, "is doing well."

A: I used an herbal tea. I don't remember the brand. But, I used that *and* a diuretic.

Q: How was the tea?

A: It tasted bad. But I did that and took a diuretic. Plus I drank lots of water before the test. Between all that water and the diuretic, I had to piss constantly. I must have pissed gallons. Well, I'm sure I pissed as much as I took in. I had to piss all the time. So me and some other job applicants were loaded into a van and were driven *very* slowly by this old guy who was taking us to the testing lab. We went so slow, I had to ask him to stop along the way so that I could piss. Then, as soon as we got to the lab, I walked in and said, "Where's the bathroom?" Everyone had to have known what I was doing. But, I passed the test. And you know, the ironic thing about that is I had only been using marijuana and I got tested for a job selling used cars.

(Private Interview, January 2000)

This humorous description may be more insightful about the roles of both applicant and drug-testing industry worker than first meets the eye. His words may be accurate: everyone indeed may have known what he was doing. It may well be the case that industry workers, like workers in all sectors of the economy, define their roles rather narrowly. In this case drug-testing industry workers may be doing little more than giving a test and delivering the results. Everything other than these tasks may be simply peripheral to their job description, their definition of it, and their worldview. Such workers may have no interest in what happens before or after they carry out their assigned duties. Their assignments may be defined as the only ones relevant to the industry occupation that they hold, such as "urine sample collector," "urine courier," or "testing technician." These front-line technicians may be as disconnected to other parts of the testing industry as automobile assembly-line workers are to each other. Their work contributes to the whole; but they may care less about a systemic completion than about their primary assignment and duty.

The courtroom work group of prosecutor, defense attorney, and judge may be similar. For this work group, quick and unimpeded delivery of "justice" is often more important than facts, evidence, alibis, and eye-witness accounts, all of which may simply slow them down and cause them more, not less, work (Walker 1985). As a result, taking care of their own specific duties, which contributes to a routinized adjudication, may be more important than other matters of the case that are not squarely relevant to their day-to-day activities.

Workers who earn their living testing job applicants and fellow workers probably are rather single-minded; they want to do their jobs as uninterruptedly as possible. Among those who actually do the testing, inquiries into whether an applicant has ingested a diuretic or a detox product may be irrelevant. Rather, the relevant and immediate concern for them is doing the testing, not snooping around or asking questions that could end up causing them more paperwork, more time invested, and more headaches, all of which most workers aspire to minimize.

I am reminded of a previous life, or at least what seems that way. Years before first entering graduate school, I was employed in state government as a social worker. Social work is a misnomer; the job required processing paper. And, it was a long way removed from the glamors of saving neglected or abused children, caring for the elderly, or delivering hot meals to the sick and needy. Rather, it entailed interviewing eight or ten people daily and determining their eligibility for food-stamp benefits. The interview itself was routine and quick—lasting about ten minutes. The next thirty minutes or so were spent doing the paperwork. I soon adopted the view of the more senior workers. The most important part of doing the job was getting the paperwork completed by the day's end. I soon didn't care if applicants were truthful or not. I didn't want to know how they were living, driving, earning, or spending money while reporting that they had no income. All that my coworkers and I wanted was a quick interview followed by routinized paperwork. We didn't want troubles, interruptions, or added work because of an inadvertently raised question or an especially troubled or emotional client. Those cases spoiled the rhythm of doing one's job. They distracted from the more important tasks—processing paper that validated clients' claims to food stamps. Such narrowly defined duties and roles, along with a desire for unimpeded work, may affect drug-testing industry workers as well.

Consider another worker/consumer's experiences with preemployment testing. His employer, a transnational paint manufacturer, tests all job applicants, including those, like him, who do not hold safety-sensitive positions. This participant reported that he nearly exclusively uses marijuana. He was and remains a stable employee, having held the job before this one for a number of years and now having worked for the paint manufacturer for more than five years. He had learned of detox products by word of mouth and had actually seen them on the shelves of a couple of local retail stores before using them.

A: When I applied, I knew they would piss test me. So, I went to this head shop and bought it.

Q: And what did you buy?

A: Vale's Original Formula.

Q: How does it work? How did you take it?

A: Ah man, the directions are pretty specific. You have to follow their schedule. You drink a bunch of water, mix the formula with water, drink it, drink more water according to their time table. Man, that stuff tasted awful too. I thought I was gonna throw it up. But, I couldn't. I just kept telling myself, "Now look, you're out of work and this just cost you thirty bucks. Don't throw it up."

Q: You managed to keep it down?

A: Yeah. And then I went on down to the Instant Clinic and pissed for them.

Q: And?

A: Well, it must have worked because I got the job.

(Private Interview, March 2000)

Barbara Ehrenreich's (2001) most recent book describes her ethnographic work within the service sector. Employed as a clerk, a maid, and a waitress, Ehrenreich details the brutalities of low-paying jobs in the service-sector economy. Subsistence pay is only part of the misery; no benefits, no grievance procedures, and nowhere else to turn comprise the harsh realities that millions of Americans, and especially women, confront as part of monopoly capitalism's transition to a temporary, service-sector economy (see, e.g., Braverman 1974: part 4). Ehrenreich describes the various tests that she was subjected to in order to secure minimum-wage-paying jobs. For example, while applying for employment at a suburban Walmart in Maine, she is instructed to take an "opinion survey with no right or wrong answers" (Ehrenreich 2001: 58). Having taken a similar test before, she sails through it but is struck with the number of questions concerning marijuana. Questions include the following:

"Some people work better when they're a little bit high," "Everyone tries marijuana," and bafflingly, "Marijuana is the same as a drink." Hmm, what kind of drink? I want to ask. "The same" how—chemically or morally? Or should I write in something flippant like, "I wouldn't know because I don't drink." (Ehrenreich 2001: 59)

Although tempted to resist corporate prying by mucking around with the expected pat answers, she instead complies with the survey. She ultimately, however, is faced with the realization that she must oppose corporate drug-testing intrusions in order to secure employment.

Sometime later, Ehrenreich applies for another Walmart job in Minnesota. She is told of the company drug-testing policy and decides, because of a "chemical indiscretion in recent weeks," to keep looking for work. "If I had used cocaine or heroin there would be no problem, since these are water-soluble and wash out of the body in a couple of days. . . . But my indiscretion involved the only drug usually detected by testing, marijuana." She compares the threat of a drug test to the dread of an approaching SAT exam and is rankled that her many virtues and positive qualities "can all be trumped by pee." Realizing that few alternatives are available, she decides to spend the weekend engaged in detoxing subterfuge.

> A web search reveals that I am on a heavily traveled path; there are dozens of sites offering help to the would-be drug-test passer, mostly in the form of ingestible products. . . . The only effective method is to flush the damn stuff out with massive quantities of fluid, at least three gallons a day. To hurry the process, there is a product called CleanP supposedly available at GNC, so I drive fifteen minutes to the nearest one, swigging tap water from an Evian bottle all the way, and ask the kid manning the place where his, uh, detox products are kept. . . . He leads me poker-faced to an impressively large locked glass case—locked either because the average price of GNC's detox products is $49.95 or because the market is thought to consist of desperate and not particularly law-abiding individuals. I read the ingredients . . . creatinine[1] and a diuretic called uva ursis. . . . I have to make myself into an unobstructed pipe: water in and water just as pure and drinkable coming out. (Ehrenreich 2001: 128–129)

Along with other innumerable workers and job applicants, Ehrenreich, quietly resists drug screening as best she can—by using detox products to affect test results.

The interesting politics of using detox products is that the resistance is one of chicanery rather than open defiance. Users intend that their resistance remain unknown to corporate and government officials. Their methods are subterranean rather than overtly political. They rebel against the internalization of the gaze and resist corporatist efforts at converting them into docile and disciplined bodies. They resist the gaze of the corporate Panopticon and in some ways are actively, but perhaps not consciously, working toward the negation of this new social order—the *Panopti-society*. Never articulating their actions in these terms, they nonetheless display this very resistance through their sly behavior.

When I first asked a friend if he would talk with me about his experiences with detox products, another acquaintance also present reacted strongly by contending, "Don't talk to him about that. It'll tip off the man." His objection to discussing the products and their experiences with them is indicative of just how quiet he and others interviewed for this research intend their resistance to remain. However, he and others in their immediate social circle who are employed and who smoke marijuana eventually acceded.

To a growing body of demanding and desperate consumers, these latest detox commodities may be viewed as a panacea that enables them to continue drug use in their private lives while maintaining job protection despite employment, economic, and political strictures.

Workers/consumers are, in the classic sociological sense, role players who fill and manage multiple and shifting roles. Within classical role theory, we are reminded that humans play dramatic parts on a stage hosting the "grand play of society" (Berger 1963: 105). As humans fluctuate among roles, they become (symbolically at least) the very masks that they slip on for their dynamic (and often transient) parts. Thus a person is publicly recognized as the embodiment of the part or mask worn for the specific role. This phenomenon is treated within symbolic interactionism as "front-stage" behavior, or impression management, which maintains privacy and conceals secrets (or back-stage behavior)—the very stuff of the dynamic theater of daily life (Goffman 1959). Each role comes equipped with a particular identity that differs from that of other characterizations. As a result, a person's life or biography unfolds as a shifting, tangled web of parts and identities. Life consists of ongoing stage performances played to vastly different audiences and with a changing cast of characters. In each case, the grand play of society demands that the role player become the part(s).

Rather than a unidimensional, psychological entity, role theory imagines the self as fluid, complex, contradictory, and unpredictable (although with some degree of expected consistency). In other words, the self *becomes* through process and is constantly shaped and refined within distinct social settings of interaction. Although some may assume that we can actually ascertain who a person really is, we find that persons are little more than things or characters within specific social situations or contexts. For most people, there is, by necessity, some consistency among the divergent roles and their particular identities. This consistency culminates, to some extent, in who the person really is (Berger 1963: 107).

There are exceptions, however, as individuals occupy vastly different, indeed contradictory, roles. In those cases individuals must use extraordinary measures to ensure that one role remains segregated from another (e.g., the role of office philanderer must remain separate from and perhaps unknown to the role of devoted husband and family man). To accomplish this, individuals rely on social-psychological mechanisms, generally referred to as neutralization techniques. These techniques allow one to engage in deviant behavior, for example, while avoiding developing a deviant self-perception. Neutralization techniques allow one to rationalize one's actions while negating any associated guilt (see, e.g., Sykes and Matza 1957).

Regarding contemporary drug use and work, individuals typically compartmentalize their public working lives from their private drug use and construct roles specific to those social settings. They manage to keep such worlds separate in part by elaborate processes. Some conceal their drug use; some discover like-minded coworkers and settle into drug-using subcultures; others abstain until testing measures are satisfied. Still others use products designed to produce false negatives. Once initial preemployment drug tests are satisfied, the majority of workers are free to go about their private drug use with little fear of subsequent testing (i.e., unless they appear inebriated or are involved in an accident while on the job). Given the degree of anonymity in contemporary, urban, organic workplaces and communities, such role segregation is relatively easy (as long as one can safely minimize the scrutiny of social surveillance and control mechanisms). Role separation probably is less successfully pulled off in smaller, rural, mechanical communities. In these settings, neighbors know their neighbors' business. Successfully deceiving others is highly improbable. Pretending to be something that one is not in those situations is unlikely to succeed. If revealed, deception may well have consequences far greater than those within less personal spheres.

Individuals juggling a number of roles are not totally free to switch or to necessarily create new ones. There are controls in place. We all live within the realities of a Durkheimian structure, its shifting social control and cold hierarchical social order. Social creatures are managed and controlled in other ways as well. To some extent, each contributes to docility and—an ideal among societies desiring to restrict large numbers of individuals—self-control.

Any social order is maintained by both formal and informal controls. States maintain social order using a number of formal or rational-legal methods. State violence remains the most extreme and final method or solution as it lurks in or threatens from the background. Yet, in the main, social control is maintained by using far less formal and physically harmful measures. For example, economic pressures usually are highly successful controlling measures. Threats to one's livelihood, prospects of finding work, or prospects of keeping or losing a job, even when subtlely made, are persuasive forces that work powerfully well. After all, casual drug users have ceased drug use, in some cases, when their employers use random drug testing. In some instances of drug use and testing, controlling behavior by threatening one's livelihood has proven successful.

Primary groups also exert pressure on individuals to conform. The powerful negative features of ridicule, gossip, and persuasion are compelling controlling influences and play significant roles in maintaining social control. With innumerable Americans accepting the possibility of a "drug-free workplace," informal, lateral pressures to cease drug use, at least while on the job, are applied to coworkers. Ridicule, informal threats, gossip, and the most serious—ostracism—are highly effective controls within some contemporary work sites. None requires physical threat. Other than the financial ones, these order-maintenance devices are laterally rather than hierarchically applied.

Control, Conflict, and Role Playing

Given the realities of structural hierarchies, perhaps none is more powerful than the social class system. It is commonly recognized that social classes live differently, both quantitatively and qualitatively. The privileged possess both economic and social capital. Their reputations are established and well credentialed. The working and lower classes possess far less, quantitatively and qualitatively. They have less social capital. Their reputations are questionable and they possess far fewer credentials. Class location and the class structure theoretically determine one's social conditions and worldview. Although some role shifting takes place across all classes, definitions of the possible are restricted by the realities of one's economic and social capital.

Yet individuals do transcend these strictures. For example, those within lower and working classes often engage in activities that are subversive to the class system and to capital's efficiency. Individuals occupying diverse roles muck around with social order, monitoring, surveillance, and control, as is witnessed by a number of human activities. People participate in such events oftentimes without attempting to necessarily transform social order—to control or negate it—but rather to make unique use of the very features of social events and controls and manipulate them to their benefit.

Goffman's (1961) observations of mental hospital patients "working the system" to their own advantage is instructive. He notes that individuals use the system in ways not officially approved or designed but for their personal benefit. Regardless of the setting, whether hospital, prison, university, or factory, people figure out ways to make it work, at least some of the time, to their advantage. Human ingenuity makes it possible to subvert control systems and to occasionally break free from the girds of cultural constraints.

In working the system, individuals also engage in "role distance," which means playing a role, as in acting, tongue-in-cheek, with little commitment to the part (Goffman 1961). One is engaged in role distance when one plays the part with an ulterior purpose. This charade or duping allows one to maintain some degree of human privacy and dignity while only superficially engaging in expected and approved types of behavior (Berger 1963: chapter 6). An example is Orwell's characters in *1984* who participate in "Two Minutes Hate," all the while doubting the actual existence of the very organization that they demonstrably hate (Orwell 1949: chapter 1). In these cases, a role is deliberately played without any personal commitment to or belief in it. In other words, the actor has no personal identification with the part. This is possible because the player has established an inner distance between his/her true identity (or that defined as true) and the role playing. Although roles typically are acted out without reflection as individuals with little forethought casually ease into and out of parts, in this case there is careful and methodical thought as one slips into a role to con another.

This explanation seemingly applies to workers who, since there has been a social class known as "workers," always have managed, in one way or another, to dupe their employers and superiors. More than likely, this has been the case in every industry and within both blue- and white-collar jobs and within both private and public sectors. Workers discover and use shortcuts; they feign being busy; they slow down various tasks; some hide on the job; others find ways to engage in sexual activities on the job; still others secretly drink or use drugs.

Regarding drug use, most drug-using employees do not desist solely because an employer implements a drug-testing policy. This is an especially reasonable surmisal since most companies using drug screening rely primarily on preemployment testing. Applicants who play the role of "clean and reputable worker" do so by stopping use for a time or opting for a method or detox product that they hope will produce a negative test result. With any luck, they then appear as drug-free prospective employees—a role that they willfully play for the benefit of their potential employer and for their own financial and other interests. Through the successful passage of this one screening measure, they essentially have established a partial reputation. After being hired, they continue the reliable, drug-free employee part while compartmentalizing their casual drug-using counterpart as separate from their on-the-job role. Playing a part for "the man," they engage in role distancing. This performance is not that different from their supervisor's behavior as he segregates his role, for example, as a drunken patron at local strip clubs from that of reputable plant manager.

Denton's critical work (1990), which differentiates the Official World from Society, is instructive. The Official World refers to formally recognized sociological facts such as institutions, organizations, ideology, roles, and role players. Society, on the other hand, is that thing raised in action as people do things together (see, e.g., Becker 1986). It is the Official World that works through its machinations to control Society, or people engaged in their activities. Formal social controls, while effective and increasing in scope, do not entirely limit individuals' behavior; otherwise deviance would be a historical topic of study. Individuals, through a host of processes and interactions, subvert the Official World and its controlling methods and procedures. People also work toward freeing themselves from assorted cultural and structural controls central to the maintenance of the Official World in order to construct a society for them and their needs. As individuals and groups actively work toward freeing themselves while using a variety of methods, they ultimately subvert social controls of the Official World.

As the Official World "demands compliance with role expectations, organizations, and the rules and laws that support them," people nonetheless are left to meet needs and satisfy their wants (Denton 1990: 141). To accomplish this, individuals disobey, ignore, or subvert the cultural constraints of the Official World, such as those governing drug use, as they create the means to secure gainful employment while continuing to casually use illicit drugs. Detox products and procedures, for many, are the means by which they do just that.

Casual drug users who rely on various products and techniques for producing false-negative drug-screening results clearly are engaged in behavior contrary to the Official World's formally approved conduct. Their role distance allows them to get what they need or want (viz., employment, a steady paycheck, and as a result, to consume). Through acts of disobedience or subversion, individuals create social-psychological mechanisms for neutralizing negative images of themselves (e.g., neutralization techniques). They do this most commonly by "(1) presenting an image to others" suggesting they are complying with dominant constraints when they actually are not; "(2) establishing relationships in which" their deviant behavior will be tolerated; and "(3) staying away from those who would react negatively to [their] actions" (Denton 1990: 145). These three techniques are briefly described below.

The first technique, presenting an image, essentially means duping or lying to others by creating a false impression of oneself that appears to be one of obedience and acquiescence—workers appearing as drug-free employees, for example. Individuals using this technique are engaged, in other words, in constructing a false image of themselves or in role distancing to appease others. By learning the techniques of projecting a specious impression, individuals minimize negative reactions of formal and informal controls of the Official World. As control techniques extend into various realms and activities of social life (e.g., selling one's car, buying a gun, flying on a passenger plane, securing a job), individuals may find themselves having to do more lying to those in positions of official control in order to navigate through life while meeting needs and satisfying wants.

Deceiving, lying, or producing a false image of oneself is also easier within the arena of the Official World than within the arena of Society. Within the Official World of work, for example, relationships are formal and hierarchical. Yet within Society, relationships are more intimate, transparent, and dynamic. One can get tripped up by lying to family, friends, and neighbors. But one often and easily can dupe representatives of the Official World. (Contrast, for example, the difficulties of having a sexual affair with one's married neighbor to the ease of federal income tax evasion.) Lying can also cause harm to relationships in Society, whereas being caught in a lie in the Official World produces few relationship problems; it may, however, result in expulsion or in other forms of formal sanction (e.g., being fined, taxed, or dismissed from a job or country club).

The second technique for containing negative reactions to deviance is to establish and maintain relationships with those who do not condemn one's deviant behavior. Such relationship building typically relies on one discovering and making acquaintance with others who are like minded. For example, those who keep their children out of public school and educate them at home, who rip out their demanding, manicured lawns and plant native grasses and flowers, who travel from dry to wet counties to purchase alcohol, who seek out an ounce of pot, and who circumvent U.S. laws to purchase banned Cuban cigars invariably gravitate toward others who are engaged in similar activities. Over time they may build communities of sorts. They become acquainted, friendly at times, and discover a safe haven where deviance (by the Official World's definition) is not only tolerated but encouraged; indeed, not deviating is often frowned upon within such subcultures. By constructing relationships apart from the Official World, role players are transformed into humans. Relationships with individuals who are simply filling roles are formed as interactions with them occur on the "basis of social relationships rather than organizational expectations." This ongoing process within organizations is subversive and serves to turn the "structure of the Official World . . . into a resource for Society" (Denton 1990: 151). As a result, workers who also happen to be casual drug users will probably, over time, find other like-minded humans occupying roles within the workplace. Stories will be shared not only about work and official work roles but also about using and procuring drugs and perhaps negating drug tests. Individuals building such communities also may discuss their abilities to compartmentalize their lives by keeping drug use separate from their working roles. They may in fact spend part of their weekends together, casually enjoying a joint on a Saturday night, with little thought or conversation given to the weekend festivities come Monday morning. Neither drug use nor the ability to dupe the official drug tests is treated as deviant. Rather, both are wholly accepted behaviors within the intimate relationship carved out of the easily maneuverable strictures of the Official World.

The third way that individuals manage to neutralize their deviance is by keeping a safe distance from those who disapprove and who have the power and authority to sanction. Translated into everyday activities this means that contacts with representatives of official control are minimized through deliberate action. For drug users, this technique is made possible through at least two processes. In the first, by segregating one's official work life from one's drug-using life, the drug user reduces his/her chances of appearing inebriated while on the job to almost nil. If workers have learned anything during this time of zero tolerance it is to not come to work stoned. Thus, they greatly reduce their chances for additional observation, questioning, testing, and control measures. Second, developing relationships with other like-minded workers probably aids their being alerted to and staying informed about company activities of control, such as random drug tests, locker searches, or the arrival of drug-sniffing canines. A casual drug user who works in isolation from other workers probably would not learn beforehand about random drug tests. But, within a social network, one has a greater chance of hearing about drug tests with enough advance warning to engage in one method or another of subversion (e.g., going home sick for the day, using a detox product, securing clean urine, feigning inability to piss on demand). Absent relationships built by those who abandon their established roles, individuals would be completely alone to confront the control methods and procedures of the Official World (Denton 1990: 153). These actions allow workers to construct a society as they behave as individuals rather than as prescribed role players. Through acting together, people engage in a quiet resistance as they subvert the gaze of the Official World's growing body of rules, regulations, and controls. Orwell's characters are again illustrative: Julia refuses to believe in any type of "organized revolt against the Party, which was bound to be a failure. . . . The clever thing was to break the rules and stay alive all the same." Julia's partner, Winston,

> wondered vaguely how many others like her there might be in the younger generation—people who had grown up in the world of the Revolution, knowing nothing else, accepting the Party as something unalterable, like the sky, not rebelling against its authority but simply evading it, as a rabbit dodges a dog." (Orwell 1949: 109)

Today, young people may not be engaged actively and overtly in efforts at ending drug testing. They are, however, quietly breaking the rules and evading corporatist drug-testing control measures. In other words, they break the rules and stay economically alive.

Efforts at duping drug tests take many forms, from using personal innovative strategies to using industry-manufactured products. Although various products and strategies for creating false-negative test results abound, employers' knowledge of such methods remains, ironically, relatively limited. This limited knowledge clearly is an advantage to job applicants and employees.

Employers and personnel officers interviewed for this research possess a blind faith in the marvels of their testing policies and procedures. Although most do not understand or care to understand the science of drug testing, they believe their detection systems are more than adequate. When corporate representatives offer information on their understanding of employees' or applicants' efforts at subverting drug-testing measures, they typically describe arcane or simplistic methods rather than more sophisticated devices or the newer diuretic products. Employers seemingly are relying on obsolete knowledge that is not in step with the changing technologies widely known within drug-using subcultures, propagated in various periodicals, and sold in retail shops and on the Internet. The following conversation with a corporate personnel officer is illustrative:

Q: I've read in the literature that there are methods by which applicants and employees will try and produce false negatives. What are some things that you are aware of that individuals use to do that and what kinds of safeguards do you have here in place to prevent that?

A: Probably the one that we're most aware of and probably the one we're most observant of would be the using of someone else's urine. Knowing that you were going to have a drug test of some kind, and carrying a vial of someone else's clean urine, maybe your own, that you did when you weren't smoking grass. And being able to slip that in, if you will, during the drug test. Now at this location, and I think in most testing facilities, the person has to give their sample. They can go obviously to the restroom, but actually in the company of another male or female person. They will actually stand there and watch them. I've heard of things, like if they put a penny behind their tongue or whatever. I've heard different things. But, I think in most cases, the results stand for what they are and it's pretty hard to determine those type of things visually. Hopefully, the testing processes are accurate enough that they can pull out that type of person. I haven't seen that much here, but in particular the random testing that I ran at another company, we would have from time to time, a diluted specimen, which they would add water. I haven't seen that here because our little cup system that we use is a pretty little simple system. Obviously with only testing for five drugs, there's things we do miss. Also because of the simplicity of the test compared to a lab test, I'm sure that the credibility of it is probably not quite as accurate as what we have in the lab.

Q: So, it's been your experience that when people try and produce a false negative that they do that by using clean urine or by diluting the sample?

A: Yes, I would say they are probably the two methods that at least I'm aware that are the most widely used.

(Private Interview, November 2000)

Notice that this company representative referred to only two methods and of course did not allude to the numerous detox products and mechanisms, or even various home remedies. Such limited knowledge of methods, procedures, products, and entire industries aimed at producing false negatives was typical among corporate spokespersons interviewed. He, like others, remained uninformed about the countless number of people who quietly use a product or procedure to negate Official World surveillance. Such methods of negation, even when subterranean, internal to one's body, and singly performed, nonetheless are modes of defiant resistance.

Ehrenreich's (2001: 134) experience was different than the monitoring described by this spokesman. At Walmart she complied with an on-site test where she was given a sample container and "sent down the hall to an ordinary public restroom. Easy enough to substitute someone else's pee, if I'd had a vial of it in my pocket or met a potential donor in the rest room," she reflects. Later, having to urinate on demand for a second service-sector job (since she, like most service-sector employees, cannot live on only one job), she is sent to a hospital and more specifically to the SmithKline Beecham Suite. After a forty-five-minute wait, a woman in blue scrubs squirts liquid soap into her hands and sends her into a private restroom. Although washing her hands prevents the use of adulterants concealed under the fingernails, she has the privacy and opportunity to substitute urine, use the Urinator, or add corporate-manufactured adulterants or neutralizing agents to her sample if she so desires (Ehrenreich 2001: 135).

Ehrenreich chose not to sabotage the test. Indeed, if caught attempting to dilute or tamper with a drug test, one can be fired from one's position or simply not hired, and in extreme instances, charged with a misdemeanor. Most individuals who use detox methods and products probably are not aware that, in some states, tampering with a drug test is a misdemeanor. And even in cases where individuals possess such knowledge, there is little evidence to suggest that they would be deterred from engaging in drug-testing subterfuge.

At this time, nine states have passed laws making cheating on drug tests illegal, with Florida and Texas leading the way. These states furthermore prohibit the production and distribution of these drug-test-duping products (Zeese 1997; "Firms offer ways" 2003). Furthermore, those states have passed criminal statutes prohibiting one from defrauding or attempting to defraud lawful urine testing. In Texas, a probationer was arrested when he arrived for a drug test for having failed an earlier one. Upon arrest, he was discovered wearing a Urinator-like device that was attached to a heat-controlled pouch containing synthetic urine. He was sentenced to a 180-day jail term for violating his probation by "possessing a phallic device to provide a false urine sample" (*Fort Worth Star-Telegram* 2002). Thus, in Florida, Texas, and other states, it is now illegal to manufacture, distribute, or use products designed to falsify drug-test results.

Drug-screening examinations occasionally produce evidence of some product or item used to cover up drug use to produce a false negative. For example, about 2 percent of positive test results in the 1999 *Drug Testing Index* showed evidence of substances used to adulterate or endanger specimen test results. In fact, and indicative of the low number of positive findings, more specimens tested positive for adulterants than for either opiates or amphetamines. Ironically, adulterants detected are not detox products. Rather, they most commonly are bleach, pyridinium chlorochromate, and oxidizing adulterants such as nitrites, which serve as masking agents ("Drug abuse and workplace demographics" 2001; *Drug Testing Index* 1999).

During this research, a laboratory analyst was questioned about chicanery and the science of detecting it.

Q: Are you aware of individuals' efforts at concealing drug use?

A: Yeah. The most effective way is to adulterate the sample after it's given. Also, adding nitrites to urine is pretty effective.

Q: Are you familiar with any products that mask or flush drugs from one's system?

A: Yeah. But, drinking cranberry juice will change the pH balance, which would work. But, these detox products you mentioned, we can detect. I'm familiar with herbal teas and they just don't work. And the liquid products, well, simply drinking that much water would have the same effect. We check for specific gravity, pH balance, etc., which must fall within prescribed parameters. Those products likely would cause a sample to fall on either side.

(Private Interview, February 1999)

This scientist's opinions are similar to those of others who suggest that it is the sheer volume of liquids consumed rather than the product itself that works in producing false-negative results for drug testing. When Ehrenreich (2001: 142) received the news from Walmart that she had passed her urine test, she could not help but wonder "whether I could have gotten the same result without spending $30." One drug-testing product manufacturer, when asked about the myriad of detox products, expressed doubt about their ability to dupe drug tests by saying, "I'd hate to risk my job by relying on one of those products" (Private Interview, February 2003).

Ongoing Resistance

Innovative approaches at engineering social control are being applied to increasing numbers of occupations, employees, prospective employees, schools, city streets, and neighborhoods (Marx 1995).[2] Drug testing is a component in a long tradition of increasingly sophisticated control measures. These governing methods, including those aimed at containing crime, often are effective. On the other hand, they also nonetheless produce unintended and dysfunctional consequences (Marx 1995: 242–46). For example, property criminals often adapt in various ways to technological target-hardening mechanisms by responding in various manners, from out-maneuvering them to engaging in more destructive and violent behavior than they perhaps would have had the measures not been in place.[3] Attempting new techniques of control often generates other or new problems. For example, Denver's increasing surveillance of graffiti and its writers blew up in its face as a few large graffiti murals were replaced with hundreds of instant "throw ups." Denver's problems, or those defined as such by city authorities, increased nearly exponentially as a result of the city's efforts at engineering social control (Ferrell 1993). Similar strategies aimed at containing crime and criminals as well as detecting drug use have produced methods, procedures, and products aimed at specifically negating official control mechanisms. Evidently, no matter whether official containment is aimed at criminal or simply antisocial behavior (however that may be defined), humans seek ways of resisting and sabotaging. Gary T. Marx recently referred to these adaptations to crime control as "second-order offenses." When applied to actions generally aimed at negating social control, they are recast as *second-order behaviors*. In other words, second-order behavior is a form of resistance to the very efforts of containing behavior. Second-order behaviors are designed to subvert control measures or strictures.

Just as there are a number of ways of resisting drug testing, so there are various ways of defying all sorts of official cultural constraints. Most behavior, regardless of the object of its resistance, develops from the direct conduct of individuals innovating as action is constructed. But, there are other sorts of resistance best characterized as organizational, or at least organized by industries offering products of corporate defiance. Detox products are part of one industry offering commodities designed to undermine the rule of law.

The remainder of this chapter focuses on people's resistance to social controls other than drug testing. Attention is given to both industry-created and individually developed modes of defiance. Since this book's focus for the most part has been on industry-based or -produced resistance (such as manufactured detox products), legally produced commodities (legal for now anyway) receive attention first. Afterwards, some subterranean styles of defiance that are characterized as illegal are given coverage.

Industries of Resistance

Although this is a factual statement rather than a command, people resist. Effective resistance among disparate individuals often is not possible in the long run, especially when controls are pervasive and target millions of people. In some cases, such as with detox products, defiance becomes possible through corporate-produced and -designed items (although not always propagated as such) for the use of countless numbers of would-be saboteurs. On the one hand, resistance becomes more effective, precise, and predictable through corporate-manufactured products of defiance. On the other hand, the whole spirit of do-it-yourself enterprising is lost in the expansion of industry-generated resistance.

Beyond detox products detailed in this book, consider the following corporate-manufactured commodities of resistance to official control.

Radar detectors represent a resistance of sorts. The obvious use of a detector is to prevent being stopped and ticketed for speeding—or, in other words, to intentionally violate the law. Yet the corporate-manufactured radar detector is something more. It reflects a mechanism that allows individuals to flaunt their independence and highway autonomy. A radar detector represents a personal strategy of liberated highway driving. It is a rebelliousness to legality, to order imposed from the outside, to seemingly arbitrary rules (or those defined as such) of driving behavior that fly in the face of the call of the highway and especially of the free-spirited hellion whose damn-the-world attitude is best characterized by red lining and high-speed cruising. Radar detectors are used by millions of Americans. Legal in almost every state, their technology has steadily improved across the years. One of the newest models, the cordless SOLO, developed by Escort, is about twice the size of a car key and uses digital signal processing. The SOLO is available for a thirty-day trial or "your money back." Unlike with detox products, evidence of a failing test (e.g., a speeding ticket) is not required for a refund. With improvements, especially with cordless technology and the manufacturing of smaller devices, detectors probably will appeal to even greater numbers of Americans, particularly young, high-tech-minded drivers who may have been put off by cords swinging from cigarette lighters, the frequent and noisy "false alarms," and the bulky size of earlier models. Radar detectors, like detox products, represent corporate-designed and -marketed forms of resistance to official control measures.

Apart from detox products sold from websites, the Internet alone transports a multitude of corporate-manufactured consumer items into homes, schools, and offices using technology while selling defiance. For example, the Internet delivers all sorts of popular music as commodity and defiance. The most widespread and successful modes of Internet music delivery have been MP3, (the now defunct) Napster, and the Amsterdam-based free music service, KaZaA. The pervasiveness of these software- and music-sharing systems became apparent by even pedestrian observation when *Rolling Stone* published, as part of its biweekly "Most Played Chart," an itemized listing of the ten "Top Pirated Internet Songs." The list was provided by the now-defunct MP3, which was dovetailed into a new business—Addictive Media Development. The lists are no longer published in *Rolling Stone,* but on July 8, 1999, the list read as follows:

Top Pirated Internet Songs
1. Eminem "My Name Is"
2. TLC "No Scrubs"
3. Fatboy Slim "Praise You"
4. Lenny Kravitz "Fly Away"
5. The Offspring "Why Don't You Get a Job?"
6. Sugar Ray "Every Morning"
7. Goo Goo Dolls "Slide"
8. Various Artists "Duel of the Fates"
9. Korn "Freak on a Leash"
10. The Offspring "Pretty Fly (for a White Guy)"

There clearly are different opinions about the motivation of software designers and users as well as the future of the music business. Some camps claim that the Internet and its dynamic technologies allow the dissemination of popular music that continually is ignored by transnational corporations and their increasing monopolization of music entertainment. That camp recognizes that federal law allows individuals to copy music for their own personal use and claims that the Internet is simply another medium (like tape recording) that provides individuals access to music and the technology to share it with others. Another camp, primarily represented by the Recording Industry Association of America (RIAA), claims that Internet software programs and music sharing are copyright infringements conducted by little more than thieves. No matter. With changing technology, consumers are in the process of snatching music from behemoth corporations who, audiophiles claim, deceived them. Despite industry assurances during the forced transition from LP to CD that CD prices would decline, they have continually increased in price; the word among technologically astute music consumers is that CDs themselves probably will be phased out in the near future, forcing consumers to adopt yet another music delivery system. Consumers are, to put it mildly, cynical about the music industry.[4] Their actions have serious repercussions. Recent technological changes that have made music sharing possible led a former Intel Corporation vice-president to proclaim, "The music industry as we now know it is over" (Gomes et al., 2000). Sure enough, just a few short months after this prophetic statement, an all-star cast of rock musicians (including Don Henley, Sheryl Crow, and the Eagles) began lobbying Washington to change the recording industry rules on everything from recording contracts to copyright ownership, control of intellectual property, and corporate accounting practices (Wild 2002).

Even with lawsuits filed against Napster by the rock-and-roll band Metallica and hip-hop artist Dr. Dre, the resistance continues as tens of thousands of consumers download Napster-like software that allows them to access on-line music sharing. All they need in order to create their own CDs, which can then be played on nearly any CD player, is a computer with a CD burner and a box of CD-Rs.

Although Napster may have been rubbed out by the RIAA's legal proceedings, in recent months a host of other Napster-like on-line music-exchange services has emerged. The top five most popular music-sharing programs at this time are Audiogalaxy, MusicCity's Morpheus, KaZaA, BearShare, and LimeWire. According to those who download music, these programs are just as easy to use as Napster and support an estimated four hundred thousand users per day. To date, the RIAA has not filed suit against these servers, although given its legal maneuvers against Napster, it will (Abowitz 2001: 29). A recent issue of *Rolling Stone* summarized some of the features of these new music-sharing sights and published numbers suggesting that tens of millions of downloads already have occurred. See Table 5.1.

Major record companies, in response to the realities of music downloading, have initiated their own downloading subscription sites—Pressplay, RealOne Music, Full Audio, and Rhapsody. The monthly subscription fee ranges from twenty to twenty-five dollars. Consumers are limited in what they can download and how music can be used; they are prohibited from downloading more than two songs per artist within a given period of time (Goodman 2002). Time will tell whether consumers will choose to pay for something less than they currently get for free.

TABLE 5.1
Music Downloading by Website and Characteristics

	Audiogalaxy	limewire/ Bearshare	Music City's Morpheus/ Kazaa	Winmx
Ease of Use	Simple, but Web interface can confuse first-time users.	Requires more technical ability than Napster.	Easy to set up and use.	Hard to install, easy to use.
Total Downloads	16,859,615	10,744,675	11,094,632	1,018,825
Strengths	Songs currently unavailable will be downloaded to you as soon as they are found. Little virus risk.	Totally decentralized service— impossible to shut down.	Lots of users; lots of music.	Napster-like interface, good search features, and a large selection.
Weaknesses	Server is often overloaded.	Truly peer-to -peer, so there is no quality control. Watch for viruses.	Requires a Web interface, which can be slow. High-bit-rate files not available—not good for audiophiles. Watch for viruses.	Watch for viruses.
Can You Get Metallica's "Enter Sandman"?	Yes. Found by searching Metallica.	Easy to find, impossible to download.	Yes, easy to find.	Easy to find, including a rare long version and live versions from bootlegs, Wood-stock '99 and with the San Francisco Symphony.

Source: Abowitz 2001.

As with detox products, the politics of resistance has found its own unique form, in this case, in the midst of young people who have the technological expertise, the time, and the desire to consume popular music using unorthodox methods. The resistance to and defiance of an emerging monopoly such as the music industry is as politically savvy as concealing one's after-hours drug use from employers. In each case, the growth of new products and technologies has dovetailed with a public desire to resist in the face of increasing corporate and social-control measures. The Internet music exchange is a new industry representing a form of defiance among profiteers. As detox products become something other than only a means to get or keep a job, buying and selling pirated CDs becomes something other than simply consuming music. Both are performed through subterfuge that allows individuals, in some small way, to evade the strictures of corporations in their work and in their leisure time. In the case of popular music and detox items, unique industries have emerged to provide consumers with a product or service that allows them an alternative or another way.

Another growing enterprise and a relatively unexplored area of research is the college-term-paper industry. Although this newly emergent service has received some attention from the popular press, to date it has been given little notice from academics, other than perhaps disparate faculty complaints over cocktails. College students now have greater opportunities for obtaining written term papers for an assortment of classes than at any time previously. The term-paper industry advertises in various periodicals and on Internet sites aimed at young people; as a result, college term papers are now widely available. Ads such as "Term Paper Assistance, Listing 19,278 Quality Research Papers" and "Term Paper Solutions, the Electronic Library" appear in a variety of publications aimed at college-aged readers. "Term Paper Assistance" claims to have "served the academic community since 1969." As with the music industry, term-paper opportunities are growing nearly exponentially with Internet technologies. Junglepage.com and Geniuspapers.com now sell term papers for between ten and twenty dollars. Schoolbytes.com also markets papers with the disclaimer that it is, ahem, "a reference source." As with the growth of other subterranean industries, this one too is framed, at least in part, as resistance to a dominant order imposed on young people by college and university authorities. The resistance is also defiance, a defiance of the morality of school codes of conduct and of the dominant belief among authorities that students must work diligently and typically alone while doing their academic work. The defiance is a short-cut probably driven by hedonism as much as anything (as may well be the case with other forms of resistance described here). But the politics of the behavior cannot be summarily dismissed. A service is being provided and a product sold by entrepreneurs and corporations that allow consumers to subvert a system over which they have little control or input. Similar to workers who use illegal drugs on weekends or during their off-duty hours, students seek ways to thwart the strictures established by those in positions of power and authority. With detox products and music sharing, there is a point-counterpoint struggle for advantage. Job applicants and music consumers try to outwit employers and the music industry. In return, commodities are manufactured to prevent their chicanery. Such is the case with college term papers, as universities and colleges are purchasing a newly developed commodity. In this case, it is computer software designed to detect these Internet-purchased term papers.

Beyond music and term-paper sharing, even legitimate American politics defies public rules and procedures as it resists the machinery of exclusive policies. The most recent example occurred during the United States presidential campaign of 2000. Green Party candidate Ralph Nader was portrayed by the Democratic Party as a "spoiler." The Democratic Party diligently worked at drawing Democratic voters away from the Nader/Green campaign and back to the Democratic stronghold. Many Democratic voters, however, were unmoved, believing that the party and its presidential candidate, Al Gore, did not represent their more progressive interests. But these voters also were worried about splitting the party and handing the presidency to George Bush Jr. As a result, Green Party activists established websites whereby voters could exchange their votes with others across the country. The intent was to work the system (or as Thoreau [1849/1957] might say, "to work as a counter friction to stop the machine" or against the system) so that the Green Party could garner 5 percent of the national vote and therefore be eligible for matching federal funds in the 2004 presidential election. The first website, nadertrader.org, implored, "If you live in a swing state, contact a Gore-voting friend in a strongly Bush-leaning state and informally agree that your friend will vote for Nader while you will vote for Gore" (Cooper 2000: 79). The second official vote-exchange site, voteswap2000.com, allowed interested voters to simply log onto the site, submit their name and e-mail address, and wait to be contacted by another disgruntled voter willing to trade votes. Voters in states that clearly were going for Al Gore or George Bush Jr. agreed with their e-mail match that they would vote for Ralph Nader while voters in states that were too close to predict would vote for Al Gore.

Despite their efforts, the Green Party failed to earn its 5 percent and the United States Supreme Court, in effect, decided the election outcome.

But, the unique aspect of that election is that voters, using this new medium, were able to subvert an election system in which they had little faith (and their suspicions must have been confirmed during the election's chaotic aftermath). During the campaign, California's secretary of state, recognizing the threat to the two-party system, claimed that voteswap2000.com corrupted the voting process. As a result, the vote-swap website in California was shut down although federal law does not prohibit vote swapping, merely vote buying (Breslau 2000: 37). Even if vote swapping were prohibited nationally, enforcing a law that is violated through such casual exchanges among millions of potentially motivated voters would be nearly impossible.

During the 2000 election, voters sought out alternatives by looking beyond the strictures of politics as usual and the two-party system. Their efforts were a form of resistance to standard procedure. They stepped out of their officially prescribed roles while using aspects of officialdom to create a society in which they attempted to get the things that they needed and wanted—a third party, propagated as viable, progressive, and internationally recognized. Not an industry per se, this vote-swapping scheme nonetheless was established and managed by legitimate organizations.

Attention is next given to efforts of defiance and resistance that are peripheral to legitimate industry-manufactured items and that primarily are engaged in by disparate yet like-minded individuals acting to create and use items that allow them to get what they want and need.

Subterranean Resistance

In late August of 1998, police departments in Massachusetts and New Jersey raided what they termed a "million-dollar ring" of young people manufacturing phony driver's licenses for underage college drinkers. This scheme, which evidently had existed for years, was made possible by an unusual state policy and practice regarding driver's-license requirements. At that time Massachusetts and New Jersey were the only states that did not require a photograph on operators' licenses (*All Things Considered*, National Public Radio August 24, 1998). As a result, this small and surreptitious operation emerged, using loopholes in authorities' regulatory systems, to further circumvent official social controls on underage drinking.

The use and possession of legal drugs are illegal unless prescribed and sold according to federal and state laws. Yet almost since the inception of drug laws, individuals and groups have found ways to gain access to pharmaceuticals through illegal means. The most common legal drugs procured illegally include Percodan, Valium, Darvon, codeine, Dilauded, and Oxycontin. Most typically these are obtained by feigning illness, convincing a medical doctor to write a prescription, or buying them or a prescription for them within underground economies.

Yet, a new method of illegally dispensing and obtaining legal drugs is gaining in popularity. The authorities, not surprisingly, have taken notice. In some Mexican communities in California, for example, some retail shops are selling everything from cosmetics to Valium. Sales clerks prescribe whatever is requested without doctors or pharmacists. Pharmaceuticals such as tetanus medicine, steroids, antibiotics, Valium, birth-control pills, and Viagra are sold in those retail stores. Drugs no longer available in the United States and those not yet approved for sale also are sold there.

Authorities claim that these shops are growing in number. Sales are booming and profits are high. Most customers are unsuspecting immigrants, who perhaps are unfamiliar with pharmaceutical regulation. Given anti-immigrant policies in California and elsewhere, they also may be marginalized from legitimate modes of consumption and, as a result, seek subterranean ones. Illegal pharmacies exist in Asian and eastern European communities as well, but are paled by their number in Hispanic communities (Haynes 1999).

The emergence of this subterranean industry represents resistance on two levels: the shop owners resist legitimizing their businesses as a way of subverting the legal machinery and regulatory oversight of government agencies. Customers resist what they may perceive as anti-immigrant hostility and states' inability (or unwillingness) to provide them with medical care. In each case, merchants and consumers have found their own way to respond to the strictures of the pharmaceutical and health-care oligarchies.

Other subterranean enterprises have emerged that, although illegal, nonetheless are political acts of resistance and defiance. They also may be considered greedy entrepreneurship. In New York, Maryland, Atlanta, Columbus, Ohio, and places abroad, including China, Italy, Greece, Germany, Japan, and Mexico, pirated-CD retailing is increasing by leaps and bounds. Investigators from the Recording Industry Association of America (RIAA), along with local police departments, have stepped up their efforts at detecting and shutting down pirate-CD operations. But, due to the availability of sophisticated technology whose prices have dropped significantly in recent years, a pirating operation can produce several hundred bootleg CDs in a given day. Like any segment of the underground economy, though, such operations are only possible when there is a consumer base, and in the case of CDs, consumers are happily paying ten dollars below retail prices. The CDs are burned onto CD-recordables or CD-Rs, which cost about one dollar each. Labels and packaging have an authentic appearance; the product is shrink wrapped and sold on street corners by street vendors or retailers. In most cases, both merchants and consumers know the CDs are pirated (Boehlert 1999). No one minds, for in this case, the ingenuity of entrepreneurs and the bargain shopping of consumers coalesce into an economic exchange that makes everyone happy. That is, everyone but the recording industry.

Within pockets of the United States, and especially urban areas, illegal micro radio stations broadcast despite threats from, and occasional raids by, the federal government. Micro stations use low-wattage broadcasting to beam their signals directly to communities. One stated concern among the majority of station workers is that legitimate radio ignores community interests; legitimate radio is homogenous, corporate minded, and profit driven.

One significant problem is that radio is becoming monopolized, which was made possible when Congress deregulated radio in 1996 with the passage of the Telecommunications Act. Before the passage of the act, the existing laws restricted a single broadcasting corporation from owning more than forty radio stations. After the act, we find that increasing numbers of radio stations are now owned by fewer and fewer large corporations. Today the "conglomerates Clear Channel Communications and Infinity Broadcasting, which built their empires after the 1996 Telecommunications Act," control most of all major markets. Clear Channel "owns more than 1100 stations nationwide, covering 247 of the nation's 250 largest markets" (Kot 2001: 26).

Clear Channel's might was widely recognized and criticized during the first few days after the September 11th (2001) terrorist attacks on New York City and Washington, D.C. Clear Channel and station programmers issued recommendations to their corporate disc jockeys that pop songs defined as "too offensive" not be played. The songs included James Taylor's "Fire and Rain," Cat Stevens's "Peace Train," the Beatles' "Obla Di, Obla Da," John Lennon's "Imagine," and everything by Rage Against the Machine. Two days after Clear Channel's actions were made public, a strident Neil Young, sporting a cowboy hat and performing for one of the several post–September 11 televised events, launched into Lennon's "Imagine."

Micro radio operators claim that their stations fill a void created by corporate radio. Micro stations broadcast music never heard on corporate radio; they broadcast community news and events and they often are overtly political in interpreting community and city activities. They often broadcast criticisms of local authorities, the police, and, of course, federally supported and sanctioned radio.

Little is required to operate a micro station: a low-wattage amplifier and a small antenna coupled with a desire to defy authorized radio protocol (see, e.g., Ferrell 2001: chapter 4). These stations are so small that they can operate anywhere, even on the move, for example, inside a van.

The Federal Communications Commission (FCC) has threatened for years to seek out, prosecute, and shut down micro radio stations, but with little success. There is little likelihood that the Feds can actually enjoy sustained success in locating and closing down such small, mobile, and community-supported enterprises. As a result of the proliferation of these stations, their local support, and the difficulties of shutting them down permanently, the federal government decided to change its strategy. The FCC, with some pressure from Congress and faced with the realization that micro stations were not going to go away, offered operating licenses to those stations that would come forward and apply. The low-power initiative developed by the FCC was a response to the 1996 Telecommunications Act, which allowed consolidation among the largest corporate radio station owners ("Congress moves" 2001). Some micro station operators were initially willing to apply for licenses. But others stated from the beginning that they had no interest in becoming legitimized by the federal government. They preferred continued defiance. Nonetheless, it seemed that once-defiant micro stations were about to be certified as legitimate. But, in December 2000, Congress voted to turn down licensing to the hundreds of tiny, low-wattage local radio stations. Congress slipped the measure into unrelated budget legislation to avoid a floor debate and a promised then–President Clinton veto. The low-wattage local stations continue broadcasting illegally and in defiance of federal regulation. This open act of resistance is much like other examples illustrated in this chapter.

Low-wattage micro radio is not the only pirate radio. Short-wave radio has its share of pirate stations. Indeed, one of the most popular periodicals on short-wave radio, station format, and location, the monthly *Monitoring Times,* features the column "Outer Limits: The Clandestine, the Unusual, the Unlicenced." The commentary features pirate short-wave stations, their formats, and their time and frequency of broadcasting (as well as broadcasting frequency in kilohertz). Also given mention are station names and the distance of their broadcasts. This is yet another form of open defiance and perhaps celebration of such as the reputable and legitimate periodical openly reports on the subversive tactics among unlicenced operators.

Conclusion

The explanation here implies a different analytical model than that used in chapter 4. A dialectical perspective on this issue shows the most promise for a holistic appreciation of contemporary control and resistance. To explain only the vast and seemingly impenetrable systems of control is to explain only part of the issue. The other issue—resistance among individuals doing it themselves or by using industry-manufactured products of defiance—is equally important. Focusing on both control and its antithesis is the essence of a dialectical explanation. The dialectic allows for a rich appreciation of both increasingly entrenched corporatist control and individuals' personal and organized resistance to it. Both simultaneously occurring control and resistance are possible and, as the data show in this manuscript, both are at work in the lives of ordinary people going about their daily affairs. A system that produces measures such as drug testing as part of larger social-control initiatives is often confronted by people working to subvert systemic manipulation of themselves and their lives. This dialectic—an organized system confronted by dynamic processes of individuals and their loosely organized resistance—offers an explanation linking the theoretical models explicated in chapter 4 to those described in this chapter.

In Hegelian terms, the dialectic "breaks down the fixity of concepts" by showing that the social contains and presupposes its opposite (Hegel 1807/1931; Norman 1976: 123). Thus, change in social-control policies and procedures, like any historical change, exhibits a dialectical movement or progression as parties negate what their oppositional parties have done or are attempting to do. In terms of drug testing and defiance, the process resembles a point–counterpoint jockeying for advantage as one side's objectives and technology are designed to outwit the other's, and on and on. The dialectic illuminates the conflict by recognizing, for example, a Foucaultian or Weberian social-control explanation on the one hand and efforts at negating it by social-psychological explications on the other.

Other than the dialectic, drug testing and detox industry products are symptomatic of capitalism's internal drive toward commodification and the logic of capital accumulation. Commodification, or capitalism's unique ability to convert everything and anything into an object for buying and selling, has been the subject of primarily historical and critical scholarship. Commodification refers to the process by which goods and services are produced and sold to consumers. This method includes the transformation of commodities from their simple state of created items (of use) into products containing properties that are redefined as necessary for social existence and lifestyles. Both individuals and organizations may define a host of commodities in these terms. Furthermore, commodification produces profits (i.e., surplus value) that are extracted from exploited workers who make the goods and, as a result, the surplus value. The goods, in the case of drug testing and resistance, may have little empirical use value (i.e., they may represent false or newly created needs). The issue of new needs is often raised in the critical question, Does a social problem commensurate with massive drug-testing policies and procedures actually exist?

Commodification, unique to capitalism, is the process by which humans manufacture both tangible and symbolic items that become culturally defined as needs. As capital generates new or revised items, false (or new) needs are culturally and socially engineered. Those items are consumed. Surplus value from the labor process is generated. Profits are realized. The ironic quality to this process is that this system allows for products designed to subvert official control mechanisms or those aimed at potentially disrupting capitalism itself. The very logic of capital demands nothing less (see, e.g., Tunnell 1992b; Wallerstein 1983). Nothing is exempt from being transformed into a commodity. After all, this system produces everything from communion wafers to weapons of mass destruction. Everything and anything also can be converted from something with its own inherent use to something that is useful primarily through exchange or for-profit purposes.

Drug use as well as other types of deviance have long been regarded as serving various societal functions. Emile Durkheim (1893/1933), for example, was among the first to consider deviance a normally occurring phenomenon that functions to reinforce moral boundaries and normative behavior. A quite different take comes from Karl Marx (1867/1906) who wrote of the material functions that deviance, crime, and criminals serve in capitalist societies. For example, crime and deviance generate vast numbers of employees to control it (and increasing numbers in the private sector). Deviant behavior also contributes as much to the production of antideviance devices as labor strikes to the production of new machinery. For Durkheim, the function served the social bond. For Marx, the function served further capital accumulation.

Deviance (and especially crime) imagery and control devices (e.g., target-hardening items) are likewise converted into commodities for buying and selling (see, e.g., Tunnell 1992b, 1998). Deviance-containment goods, as commodities, evidently satisfy human wants, as consumers (in the case of drug-testing employers) increasingly define such items as necessary for their social existence—that is, as life with capitalism "becomes dominated by the passion to possess the commodity's living power" (Balbus 1977: 575). Deviance and its control, in this context, contribute indirectly to commodity production.

Commodity exchange, or the process of buying and selling, operates by its own logic, as Friedrich Engels (1878/1939: 297) aptly stated:

> Commodity production, like all other forms of production, has its own laws which are inherent in and inseparable from it. These laws are manifested in the sole form of social relationships which continue to exist, in exchange, and enforce themselves on the individual producers as compulsory laws of competition.

Thus, the motor of capitalism, of commodity exchange, is compulsory competition—competition that necessitates the creation of new needs, new consumer goods, and new uses for them. In other words, commodity production does more than simply respond to consumer needs; it creates them (see, e.g., Galbraith 1978). Industry and government were central to the origin and persistence of commodities used in testing workers and students. These vested parties contributed indirectly to the emergence of the detox industry.

A recent commentary on this component of commodity exchange demonstrates that further accumulation of capital (a systemic necessity) depends on generating increasing numbers of commodities for buying and selling.

> In the course of seeking to accumulate more and more capital, capitalists have sought to commodify more and more. Since capitalism is a self-regarding process, it follows that no social transaction has been intrinsically exempt from possible inclusion. That is why we may say that the historical development of capitalism has involved the thrust towards the commodification of everything. (Wallerstein 1983: 16)

Thus, in a system that depends on increasing accumulations of capital, everything, including deviance and social control, drug use and drug prevention, drug testing and drug-test duping, has the potential to become transposed into a commodity. As commodity production seeks new objects for buying and selling as well as new markets, the various dimensions of deviance—as threat, as imagery, as entertainment, as news, and as a challenge to defend against—increasingly are included in the production processes and transformed into commodities.

This explanation also is clearer when one uses the dialectic, which treats commodity production as the impetus for analysis, as a method of examining such recent and contradictory developments. Dialectical interpretations situate a phenomenon's change within the dynamics of production—in this case, commodity production or capitalism. The contradictory nature of commodity production is essential for explaining social life, consciousness, and drug-control commodities in contrast to the financial costs of containment (given the small number of positive findings). These contradictions have at their core the fundamental incongruities between use value and exchange value—the heart of Marx's dialectic (see, e.g., Fisk 1979; Somerville 1967). Not only are exchange and use values contradictory; they are in opposition, contributing further to advances in the production of goods and services whether needed or not and whether justified or not by any social demand or use (see, e.g., Meikle 1979). The drug-containment and -control commodities described in this book seemingly contain less use value than their presence suggests; they are less necessary for our social welfare than corporate consumers may believe. Their material value lies in their exchange, made possible by capitalism's ability to create and market goods and services with little regard for their need (see, e.g., Marx 1867/1906), the result of which is further capital accumulation. Other theoretical perspectives might prove useful for such an analysis, but the emphasis here is on the commodification process or the contradiction between use and exchange value.

According to Engels (preface to *The Communist Manifesto*, Marx and Engels 1948), "all history has been a history of class struggles or struggles between exploited and exploiting, between dominated and dominating classes at various stages of social development." Indeed, this is obviously the case with conflict between such groups as workers and corporate owners; citizens and their governments; micro radio broadcasters and the centralized FCC; music downloaders and the RIAA; bicyclists taking back the streets and government-sanctioned automobile drivers; and street people and corporatist controllers of cultural space (see, e.g., Ferrell 2001). Some old, some new, these conflicts engage distinct groupings of people who have widely vested yet different interests at work. The one commonality is that one side of each conflict is dominant (whether public or private). These conflicts, just like the ones described in this book between corporate/government policy and workers/applicants, embody the dialectic. For policies governing work and social control of the dominated (workers, applicants, students) are in a state of constant motion or change. The opposed forces at work produce new forms of social relations. In other words, peoples in conflict (which is a normal state of society) produce an ever-changing, dynamic society. Thus, conflict over drug testing in the workplace has resulted in changes in the production of certain goods and modes of chicanery. The dialectic stresses the contextualization of the phenomenon being explained. In this case, to appreciate the emergence of the detox industry one must situate it in the rise of drug testing in the workplace and government policies that support such. As drug testing in the workplace took hold, in small, incremental steps, through court rulings, executive orders, and legislative actions, just as slowly did the detox industry emerge. A dialectical interpretation focuses on these small, quantitative changes that ultimately led to qualitative change—in this case, to the formation of a new multi-million-dollar detox industry fueled by workers desiring to secure and maintain employment. In this way, the dialectic demands an historical interpretation, as antecedents are understood as sufficient to produce changes elsewhere.

As Marx described the commodity as having inherently contradictory characteristics (viz., regarding use and exchange value), we witness newly emerging styles of social control containing within them their own "seeds of destruction." In the case of drug testing, "destruction" may be an overstatement. But, defiance as practiced through subversive methods is certainly a contradictory component of social control. Other types of resistance on many fronts described in this chapter represent the same. Corporatist policies of drug testing applicants and employees have resulted in the very products and strategies for making control measures less effective; they allow drug-using employees and applicants to behave in ways other than those imagined and intended by state and corporate managers.

Given that postmodern society is characterized as a consumer-driven society, the dialectic also includes the other side of commodification—consumption. Beyond the forces of commodity production, the forces of consumption permeate postmodern societies. Forces of consumption are those behemoth organizations and industries of advertising, shopping malls, shopping television networks, the Internet, and mail-order firms. The marketplace is glutted with industry-manufactured drugs and drug-testing commodities. Just as pervasive are those consumables of drug-testing defiance, as a simple Internet search reveals.

Consuming these items may have little to do with conventional notions of reality. For example, when consumers purchase something, they are doing more than buying an item. They are consuming signs about what its consumption indicates about themselves. In other words, through consumption, consumers symbolically signify who or what they are, whether it be a new owner of a Jaguar, a Happy Meal, or a drug-flushing product. If the latter, then the consumption of that product is indicative of one's commitment to drug use. Symbolically at the least, consumption of a detox product represents one's recalcitrance and intentions of remaining part of a drug-using subculture unbeknownst to the boss. As social emphases shift from production to consumption, drug-testing products are consumed by corporations and government agencies and their antithesis by employees, job applicants, and, increasingly, students. According to Merton's observations of several decades ago, "Some social structures exert a definite pressure on certain persons in the society to engage in nonconforming conduct rather than conformist conduct" (Merton 1938: 672). Social structural restrictions include those of employment, licensing, and legitimate arenas of consumption—in other words, entrenched organizations and social institutions.

But, any detailed attention to nonconformist conduct and resistance must consider more than social structure, as formidable as it is. Although Max Weber gave great attention to issues of social structure, his was a sociology that focused especially on humans doing things together, or human action. Although he wrote at length about societies and bureaucracies, Weber's interest was in the process of human interaction. In particular, Weber's "value-rational action" and his "means-end rational action" are especially salient to this issue of human resistance to social control. Resistance, even passive resistance, is action. Value-rational action pertains to humans behaving in a manner that is determined best for some larger set of values or group rather than solely for the good of the individual. Thus, resistance to drug testing for many may be action that is part of a larger plan or strategy to negate testing policies. Groups of workers actively participate in undoing testing rules and procedures for the good of something public rather than individual. To that end, their individual values or preferred styles of acting may be overshadowed by their loyalty to a collective or organized response to drug testing.

Another way of thinking about workers' actions is centered on the realization that they are actors within a particular social class who, perhaps, could be viewed as behaving in relation to their class-based interests. There likely are differing interpretations of and opinions on the issue of explaining workers' subterfuge as some form of class-based consciousness. Some may treat workers' activities at duping employers, regardless of the depth or breadth, as a crude class consciousness in action. In this scenario workers are potential rebels against ownership, the wage system, inequalities, and centralized, corporate surveillance. Other camps counter these interpretations and suggest that workers, in the case of drug testing, are engaged in little more than economic survival and hedonistic behavior. The differing interpretations treat workers theoretically as both antisystemic class players and hedonistic individualists with little or no political consciousness. The reality, from evidence to date, may actually reside somewhere in between.

Most politically conscious actors, whether functioning to benefit solely themselves or a collective, possess an awareness or consciousness of their plight, ultimate aspirations, and the strategies for linking their objectives to action. In other words, they exhibit a consciousness about their reality and goals and commit themselves to strategies that reconcile the distances between them. Unlike consciousness that is manifest in more sophisticated political action, however, workers may display a form of consciousness manifest in drug-testing duping with little recognition and articulation of political aspirations and strategies.

Workers, in this case, may not be able to recognize the politics of their actions; their attention may be fully committed to the immediacy of their wants and needs in the presence of their lived realities of working for a wage, concealing their drug use, and finding few decent jobs (with their limited social capital). It may well be the case that consciousness among workers, even though largely unrecognized by the actors themselves, may represent a different manifestation of politicized action from that more commonly demonstrated by conscious workers found within market societies.

Given the stated social objective of zero tolerance, drug-using workers realize that few options exist for them to maintain their desired lifestyles. In fact, in many cases, continued drug use may be that preferred course of action, especially given workers' commitment to drug-using subcultures, autonomy, and hedonism. Yet, such preferences may have little to do with their subterfuge as politics-in-action. In any event, workers rarely explain their situations in such terms. They rely instead on personal strategies to solve what they define as personal problems.

Unlike class- or group-conscious workers engaging in resistance for the common good, their behaviors resemble Weber's "means-end rational action." This more than likely applies to the majority of drug-testing saboteurs. In this case, the actor is not driven by a larger value system, its ideologies or strategies. Rather, actors using means-end rational action pursue their own objectives. This pursuit is not asocial; it is shaped by the environment within which one finds oneself. Actors must determine the best way, given their circumstances, of getting what they want. Recognizing that these types of actions are ideal types, actors rarely if ever operate solely within one style. And regardless, the politics of workers' actions or inaction cannot be summarily dismissed.

Some might characterize this defiance as a form of edgework (see, e.g., Lyng 1990). Although there is an element of excitement and adrenalin rush in the very act of defiant urination (or pissing on da man) this likely is not edgework per se since there is little foreground edge to the act. Rather, the defiance arguably occurs in the background as actor prepares for the act. There, in one's basement apartment or family bathroom and isolated from other drug users, does it begin through flushing, for example. The act of defiance, the politics of subterfuge, begins and largely occurs in the background to pissing on demand.

Politics without a stated consciousness of political act is present in lived experiences. Nonetheless, we must recognize some level of political deed in this mode of subterfuge, especially given that role distancing by necessity persists over several days. Typically occurring acts of resistance that most readily come to mind are more immediate and short-term behaviors. But detoxing for duping drug tests implies a commitment to a strategy of subversion for the long haul, or at least for a few days. Something political is going on here.

It is neither obviously political nor solely hedonistic. In fact, it is neither and both. Yet again, we see that the dialectic is useful, for it recognizes the fluidity of the issue and the interstices of motivational meaning. When asked, "Political or personal?" it answers, "Yes."

Today the dialectic is most commonly understood as a postmodern analytic device. It is especially useful when confronting ambiguity. Postmodernism celebrates too that the personal is political.

There is nothing so personal as peeing. Even when humans are forced into public places for relieving themselves, they nonetheless try to maintain some dignified privacy. Even when men are forced to share a common trough, there is some effort made to not see and not be seen. But when one is coerced into pissing on demand by employers whose policies are supported by the state, the act becomes political. Observed, forced urination by an employer for a job is akin to extortion. This strong-armed behavior is a politicized act. Complying with or defying the legitimated process of extracting pee is also a politicized act.

Groups of workers, functioning as a group rather than as disparate individuals, are organizing and challenging drug-testing policies and their implementation. There is no indication of a class-based consciousness per se but there is a collective spirit at work as workers set aside differences and divisions and challenge workplace controls. Their objectives transcend individual hedonism.

During the early days of workplace drug testing, the new rules and procedures were challenged at every turn, by labor lawyers, labor unions, workers, and political interest groups, whether conservative, liberal, or libertarian. But as testing processes became improved, as the number of false positives decreased, and as policies were revised, refined, and upheld by courts and labor boards, workers came to accept the realities of workplace drug testing. Few political challenges to testing occurred during the latter two-thirds of the 1990s (see, e.g., Gilliom 1994) other than those to student testing. But, during the summer of 2001, State Department employees, calling themselves the Defenders of the Fourth Amendment, challenged the federal government's policies on random drug testing by claiming that testing is not a cost-effective deterrent and is an unwarranted invasion of privacy. The Defenders of the Fourth Amendment are especially concerned about the testing of employees who do not participate in national security issues and thus are not in safety-sensitive positions.

They point out that the federal government's random testing costs $10.7 million annually and produces four hundred positive results out of 1.8 million workers. From 1993 to 1998, the federal government conducted 257,576 random tests and discovered 1,345 positive cases, or 0.52 percent of those tested. The six years of random testing cost taxpayers a total of $31,791,811. Each positive finding cost a whopping $23,637.

Federal officials claim that drug-testing programs serve as a deterrent to drug use. Yet, the Defenders counter the deterrent claim by showing that positive test rates have remained constant from 1987 to 1996. Testing opponents use such figures in their argument that random testing, in this case, is neither cost-effective nor a deterrent. Were it a deterrent, they argue, the percentage of positive results would have fallen rather than remained constant across the ten-year period (Nakashima 2001).

Resistance to drug testing and other realities of public life continue on other fronts as well. The politics of pissing on demand continues. We hear of it so infrequently that we easily assume it does not occur. Yet, it is precisely the silent type that well may be the most effective at negating social containment efforts. Silent protest or quiet politics is still political protest.

Whether corporate-manufactured or individually initiated, resistance is an ongoing feature of social life.

Postscript

Dave Lee, having last used illicit drugs twenty-five years ago, complied with the corporate demand and produced a strong, clean, soldier's stream. He now flies the friendly skies and pulls in a military pension to boot. Recalling her recent indiscretion, Hannah slipped off to her local GNC. After several gallons of water over three days, a B vitamin, and a blackberry-flavored dose of resistance, she complied and produced a good, clean stream. I know you've seen her down at your local Walmart, where she works as a minimum-wage-earning clerk.

Appendix

As with most authors and their work, the idea for this book occurred by happenstance. And as with many researchers, I did not discover this topic while perusing the stacks of a university library, attending professional conferences, or discussing abstract notions of philosophy and science. No, like many research ideas, this one evolved through casual observation and conversation beginning one evening over a few drinks with friends. One particular friend, a few months prior, had been laid off from work. He had been looking for a job (mainly blue collar) but was selective because of the pay scale to which he'd become accustomed. He had an upcoming interview, so he told me, with a transnational manufacturing company, and was hoping to land the job. For him, there was just one slight problem—the company policy requiring preemployment drug testing. Although my friend had been out of work for some time and clearly was not happy about his situation, and although he regularly indulged in smoking cannabis sativa, he seemed relatively unconcerned about the prospects of a urine test for work. He spoke more about "the man and how our behavior is being monitored" than about the possibility of not being hired because of a drug test. His concern was with abstract notions of growing social control evidenced by drug testing in the workplace rather than with the immediate effects of that control on his life and livelihood.

As we talked, I learned that he was in the process of becoming well prepared for his drug test. He recently had paid a visit to a local "head shop" that sells, among other items, detox products (viz., Vales and Detoxify). "Products for passing drug tests?" I inquired. And, sure enough, he later showed me the packaging and the product's detailed instructions—four pages' worth. He was in the middle of prepping for the test by drinking untold amounts of water, abstaining from using marijuana, and, in his words, "eating right." Two days later, he was ordered to a local health clinic where he had to piss, on demand and in the presence of a monitor, into a specimen cup. A couple of hours before leaving his house for the scheduled drug test, he drank down a foul-tasting glass of a powdered detox product and a vitamin B. About a day and a half later he was asked to come into the manufacturing plant and was offered the job, which, some five years later, he still holds.

As time went by, I continued asking my friend about the product that he had used and how he had learned of it. I asked how it worked and if any of his friends had used similar covert methods. I began looking around in health food stores, head shops, and drug stores at the many detox products. My pedestrian interest in these products soon shifted to doing research on the phenomenon of drug testing in the workplace; I was astounded to learn of its pervasiveness. Thus, informal conversations with my friend led me to consider other facets of drug testing in the workplace and individuals' adaptations to it. I soon came to believe that drug testing and subverting testing by using detox products was an unexplored area of scholarship and an area linking overt politics to covert defiance. As a result, I began doing more than just casually talking and observing. I began crafting a research design to study drug testing, the products used to subvert it, and the methods used by workers and would-be workers.

This research relied on both primary and secondary data. Primary data were obtained from loosely structured interviews. Face-to-face interviews took place in cities and small towns in Kentucky, Tennessee, Georgia, Arizona, and Illinois. Telephone interviews were held with various individuals located in New York, Illinois, Arizona, Colorado, Maryland, and Washington, D.C. Secondary data consists of government and industry documents.

Interviews were conducted with the various players central to understanding drug testing and its subversion. Thus, interviews (mainly formal, sometimes informal, and at other times merely conversations) were conducted with corporate spokespersons who oversee drug testing at their places of business; laboratory officials and medical review officers who analyze urine samples and discuss their findings with those who yield the samples; corporate spokespersons in the drug-testing industry; manufacturers of the various detox products; retail merchants who sell detox products; and consumers who use the products. With this type of research it often is difficult to draw a fine line of distinction between formal interviews and casual conversations. Indeed, today, thinking about the various individuals with whom I have talked, I would be hard pressed to say precisely how many conversations I've had about this topic of drug testing and subversion. Some conversations lasted an hour, others only a couple of minutes. Some discussions produced invaluable data; others produced nothing useful for this book although they may have caused me to think differently about the issue or to consider talking with other persons.

Locating some interview participants was easy. Corporate spokespersons are found at places of business and laboratory officials and medical review officers are found in the yellow pages of telephone books. Corporate spokespersons in the drug-testing industry were more difficult to talk with. But, there are only a handful of major corporations producing drug-testing devices and technologies (e.g., Syva, Abbot, Roche); thus identifying and locating them was relatively easy. Manufacturers of detox products were located by using two methods. First, while visiting local retail shops selling detox products (and talking with the retail merchants), I noted names, addresses, and phone numbers of product manufacturers. Later I telephoned them and talked with their spokespersons by phone and some, at later dates, face to face and usually at their place of business. Of the various central players for this research, these manufacturers were the most guarded, suspicious, and difficult to interview. The second method was simply searching websites by using such key search words as "drug testing" or "detox."

Consumers of detox products were also reluctant to talk, fearing that this research might "tip off the man" and make future drug-testing subversion increasingly difficult. But, consumers did talk with me, sometimes quite by accident in, for example, a bar or head shop. Other discussions were a bit more formal, but none were, in the traditional sense of the meaning, formal interviews. I located consumers by simply striking up conversations with particular people about the research and asking friends to introduce me to friends. I also had some help from members of a healthy local Dead Head community. My finding consumers to interview relied essentially on snowball sampling procedures.

Interviews with drug-testing-industry spokespersons and some detox-product manufacturers took place over the telephone. Interviews with industry spokespersons (e.g., human resource officers), laboratory officials, medical review officers, retail merchants, consumers, and some detox-product manufacturers took place face to face. Face-to-face interviews were held in four different cities in four different states (Kentucky, Illinois, Arizona, and Tennessee). Two of the cities have populations of over one hundred and fifty thousand, one a population of thirty thousand, and one a population of nearly four hundred thousand.

Each person interviewed or casually talked with was told of my intention to write something for the academic audience about this issue. Some required proof, such as a university ID or a letter in advance on university letterhead. ("You may be the media misrepresenting yourself," more than one said during telephone conversations.)

Only once did I deceive people about my identity, although no formal interviews were conducted at that time. I attended an industry trade show in Baltimore to learn more about the products and linkages between manufacturing and retail. In order to get into the trade show, I had to produce bogus credentials in the form of a phony business card. I claimed I owned a small retail shop selling vitamins, supplements, and detox products. I could not have gained entry by letting the industry trade-show officials know my real identity or purpose. No one was harmed by my duplicity and I am convinced that I did not interfere with the show, its purpose, or the many conventioneers.

Given that my research has consistently used interview methods, I have remained sensitive to issues of establishing rapport, assuring and maintaining confidentiality, and securing data. During the course of this research, I experienced few problems with making contacts or gaining cooperation from the various interview participants. The data and participants' confidentiality were always kept secure.

Throughout the course of this research, I kept field notes or analytic memos. The notes were used to make analytic sense of the data as collected; they produced a "sparking of ideas," which were written down and used for more specific data analysis (Glaser 1978; Lofland and Lofland 1984: 149). The construction of field notes in qualitative strategies constitutes an "internal dialogue, or thinking aloud" and is an activity that prevents one from making only pedestrian observations. It demands "question[ing] what one knows, how such knowledge has been acquired, the degree of certainty of such knowledge, and what further lines of enquiry are implied" (Hammersley and Atkinson 1983: 164, 165).

With qualitative research, data analysis is an ongoing process that often occurs in tandem with data collection and categorization. These simultaneously occurring events are mutually supportive and result in several levels of analysis feeding back into one another (Schwartz and Jacobs 1979: 28). Data analysis, in this case and in nearly all cases of qualitative research, relied on the concept of "constant comparison," a process of continuing verification. This process required comparing the responses and experiences of sample members to get to a point of understanding particular uniformities. To that end, similarities and differences were highlighted as patterns emerged, were analyzed, and were theoretically explained (Glaser and Strauss 1967). Field notes were vital to this entire analytical process (see, e.g., Sanjek 1990).

This research was supported in part by two internal grants from Eastern Kentucky University. The strategies and conclusions are the sole responsibility of the author and do not necessarily represent Eastern Kentucky University or EKU's Program of Distinction.

Notes

NOTES TO CHAPTER 1

1. In some cases, employees' random tests are not a complete surprise. Interviews with employees and retailers (as discussed later) indicate that employees often learn of random testing schedules in advance, which allows for ample time to ensure that they produce negative test results. Such knowledge probably plays a part in the low number of positive results from random tests.

2. Metabolites are building blocks for cells and, as organic material, they die and are discarded. Once a substance is ingested, the body metabolizes it. Marijuana and other drugs, when ingested, become part of the metabolites that die and then are expelled through urination. Drug testing examines metabolites rather than drugs per se since what is expelled in the urine is no longer the drug but subsequent inactive metabolites of it. In order for drugs to be detected in metabolites, they must have been ingested more than about one day and less than, say, one week prior to a urine test.

3. The two major federal acts, the Omnibus Transportation Employee Testing Act (Public Law 102-143; October 28, 1991) and the Drug-Free Workplace Act (Public Law 100-690; November 18, 1988) actually do not require the majority of private corporations to drug test employees or applicants. The Omnibus Transportation Act requires the testing of all workers who hold or apply for "safety-sensitive positions." The Drug-Free Workplace Act simply requires companies with federal contracts of twenty-five thousand dollars or more to demonstrate that they have made reasonable efforts at maintaining a drug-free workplace (*Drug Testing: A Bad Investment* 1999).

NOTES TO CHAPTER 2

1. The U.S. Army's policy requiring testing soldiers returning home from Vietnam was struck down in a 1974 U.S. Court of Military Appeals case. In *United States v. Robert J. Ruiz,* the military court ruled that although a testing program designed to rehabilitate soldiers was laudable, it could not "outweigh the accused's right to refuse obedience to an order, compliance with which would require him to furnish evidence that might tend to incriminate him."

161

2. This is analogous to asset forfeiture, another tool in the war on drugs, which shifts the burden of proof from the state to the accused. The burden is on the latter to prove that confiscated property was not purchased with drug money or used in the process of buying and selling illegal drugs.

3. As a point of clarification, "small businesses," as defined by nearly all business and economics texts, are independently owned and do not dominate their particular fields. Business size is sometimes determined by the number of employees and at other times by the company's annual capital.

4. Although this company, like most, does not periodically screen its employees for traces of lead or other toxic elements and chemicals used in production, it nonetheless subjects applicants to drug testing. Likewise, data from a 1999 American Management Association survey indicate that while 70 percent of applicants are tested for illegal substances, only 16.7 percent are tested for "susceptibility to workplace hazards" (e.g., exposure to toxins).

5. Regardless of its original meaning, the term "officer" in the vernacular communicates authority and power and, as a result, is understood as describing a position to be feared rather than necessarily revered. Heads of personnel and medical doctors are office holders, no doubt, but their titles and duties are being redefined within a culture of surveillance and as they increasingly serve as operatives within the ongoing war on (some) drugs (see, e.g., Staples 1997).

6. Three months later this company was sold to another and 10 percent of the work force was laid off.

7. Moral and ethical questions about the respectful treatment of nonhuman animals or their ownership are rarely broached within these industries or within broader discussions of the sociology of crime and deviance (see, e.g., Beirne 1999).

NOTES TO CHAPTER 3

1. A diuretic is anything that promotes the formation of urine. Diuretic drugs are designed specifically to cause a person to "lose water." The process by which diuretics cause urination varies, but each produces heavier and more-frequent-than-normal urination.

2. Creatine is a compound that is synthesized by the body and is then used to store energy. Energy storage occurs when phosphate molecules are attached to creatine, which creates creatine phosphate. Creatine is sold as a dietary supplement and is used by some athletes as a steroid to increase muscle bulk. Among the medical community, some concern has been expressed about the long-term effects of using creatine as a dietary supplement, especially regarding digestive, muscular, and cardiovascular problems.

3. Rinsing one's hair with a detoxing cream rinse allegedly washes away evidence of marijuana use and negates hair-testing results. Given the likelihood that

hair testing will become increasingly popular, various shampoos to wash away residue of drug use are being developed and marketed.

4. Hydroponic growing kits are devices used for growing marijuana indoors. A kit uses only water, no soil. Kits typically come with recommendations for pre-scribed grow lights and timers. The unit itself is relatively small—a foot in cir-cumference and five feet in height. It is designed to fit into a small closet, for ex-ample, so that growers can conceal the device, its timed lights, and the fruits of their labor.

5. Getting a refund is not particularly easy. Detox product users who have gotten an unfavorable result on their drug test are those who ask for refunds. Yet detox manufacturers require several items, including the product's packaging, the receipt, and the actual drug test report of a positive finding from a medical doctor or employer. These requirements, by design, may minimize refunds. A small fraction of customers ever request a refund. Such low numbers then be-come part of detox companies' boasting and advertising.

6. Ironically, these are commonly listed side effects of everything from Al-buterol to ibuprofen, each of which is wholly supported by the medical commu-nity and FDA approved.

NOTES TO CHAPTER 4

1. As an example, former President Reagan's Executive Order 12564 immedi-ately subjected all federal employees to drug testing. Few entities are likely to strike the American people as any more formal and less personal than the ma-chinery of the federal government.

2. Industry spokespersons, as described in chapters 2 and 3, claim that costs are negligible. In other cases, they admit that they do not know if on-site testing makes good economic sense. To date, there has been no published research on the cost-effectiveness of on-site testing.

NOTES TO CHAPTER 5

1. Creatinine is "a chemical waste molecule that is generated from muscle me-tabolism. Creatinine is produced from creatine, a molecule of major importance for energy production in muscles. Creatinine is transported through the blood-stream to the kidneys. The kidneys filter out most of the Creatinine and dispose of it in the urine" ("Creatinine" 2000).

2. Consider the surveillance of Washington, D.C., as earlier described. Similar closed-circuit cameras are at work in a number of American cities. Electronic surveillance is simply found everywhere in private businesses and is increasingly located in once-public space as well (see, e.g., Ferrell 2001).

3. Target hardening is a process by which individuals and organizations make

themselves and their property difficult to victimize. Their property, for example, as a target of theft, is "hardened," or made more troublesome to steal. This is accomplished by using all sorts of strategies and products. For example, individuals may change their routes when walking home late at night so as to avoid dark street corners. Or, they may carry a weapon of defense such as pepper spray or a handgun. Property owners fortify their businesses and homes with private security officers, fencing, alarm systems, motion lights, and closed-circuit cameras, for example. These products and services are (as are crime-reenactment television programs, movies, and some popular music) examples of the ongoing commodification of crime as threat, containment, and imagery.

4. A class-action lawsuit filed by attorneys general in twenty-eight states against the top five CD distributors and the three largest music retailers (in the United States) was recently settled out of court. The attorneys general claimed these companies had fixed retail prices of CDs from 1995 through 2000, overcharging consumers $480 million. The out-of-court settlement was $143 million, which will be distributed to consumers in the amount of five to twenty dollars (Tsang 2003).

References

Abowitz, Richard. 2001. "Napster: The next generation." *Rolling Stone* August 30: 29, 32.

Ackerman, Deborah L. 1991. "A history of drug testing." Pp. 3–21 in Robert H. Coombs and Louis Jolyon West (eds.), *Drug Testing: Issues and Options*. New York: Oxford University Press.

Akers, Ronald L. 1994. *Criminological Theories*. Los Angeles: Roxbury.

All Things Considered. 2002. National Public Radio. February 21.

All Things Considered. 1998. National Public Radio. August 24.

American Management Association. 2001. "U.S. corporations reduce levels of medical, drug and psychological testing of employees." New York: American Management Association.

American Management Association. 1999. "U.S. corporations reduce levels of medical, drug and psychological testing of employees." New York: American Management Association.

American Management Association. 1996. *Drug Abuse: Workplace Drug Testing and Drug Abuse Policies, 1996 Survey*. New York: American Management Association.

An Analysis of Worker Drug Use and Workplace Policies and Programs. 1997. Washington, DC: U.S. Department of Health and Human Services. July.

"Attitudes toward the most important problem facing the country." 1996. P. 114 in *Sourcebook of Criminal Justice Statistics*. Washington, DC: U.S. Department of Justice.

Balbus, Isaac D. 1977. "Commodity form and legal form: An essay on the relative autonomy of the law." *Law and Society* Winter: 571–88.

Becker, Howard S. 1986. *Doing Things Together: Selected Papers*. Evanston, IL: Northwestern University Press.

"Bedtime story." 2002. *Wellness Letter: The Newsletter of Nutrition, Fitness and Stress Management* 18 (6): 3.

Beirne, Piers. 1999. "For a nonspeciesist criminology: Animal abuse as an object of study." *Criminology* 37 (1): 117–47.

Berger, Peter L. 1963. *Invitation to Sociology*. New York: Doubleday.

Black, Donald. 1984. *Toward a General Theory of Social Control*. 2 volumes. New York: Academic Press.

Blum, T., D. Fields, S. Milne, and C. Spell. 1992. "Workplace drug testing programs: A review of research and a survey of worksites." *Journal of Employee Assistance Research* 1: 315–49.

Blumberg, Paul. 1989. *The Predatory Society: Deception in the American Marketplace*. New York: Oxford University Press.

Board of Pottawatomie County et al. v. Lindsay Earls et al. 2002. No. 01-332 Supreme Court of the United States.

Boehlert, Eric. 1999. "CD piracy: Easier than ever." *Rolling Stone* September 2: 29, 32.

Borg, Marian J., and William P. Arnold III. 1997. "Social monitoring as social control: The case of drug testing in a medical workplace." *Sociological Forum* 12 (3): 441–60.

Braverman, Harry. 1974. *Labor and Monopoly Capital*. New York: Monthly Review Press.

Breslau, Karen. 2000. "Meet Nader's traders." *Newsweek* November 13: 37.

Brooke, James. 2000. "Marijuana growers, smokers love British Columbia." *Lexington Herald-Leader* August 27: A6.

Campbell, K. K. 1995. "Pissing away." *Eye Weekly: Toronto's Arts Newspaper* April 20: 2.

Chandler v. Miller, 117 U.S. 1303 (1997).

"Characteristics of adults on probation, 1995." 1997. In *Bureau of Justice Statistics*. Washington, DC: National Institute of Justice.

Christie, Nils. 1994. *Crime Control as Industry* (2d ed.). London: Routledge.

"The claims game: The consumer loses." 2001. *Wellness Letter: The Newsletter of Nutrition, Fitness and Stress Management* 17 (7): 5.

Claims That Can Be Made for Conventional Foods and Dietary Supplements. 2001. Washington, DC: U.S. Food and Drug Administration. Office of Nutritional Products, Labeling, and Dietary Supplements. October.

Cohen, Sidney. 1983. "Drugs in the workplace." *Drug Abuse and Alcoholism Newsletter* 12 (August): 3–6.

Cohen, Stanley. 1985. *Visions of Social Control*. Cambridge: Polity Press.

Cooper, Matthew. 2000. "Just mad about Nader." *Time* November 6: 79.

"Congress moves against micro radio." 2001. *Rolling Stone* February 15: 28.

"Creatine: Behind the hype." 2002. *Wellness Letter: The Newsletter of Nutrition, Fitness and Self-Care* 18 (7): 6.

"Creatinine." 2000. *Medical Dictionary*. www.medterms.com/script/main.

Denton, John A. 1990. *Society and the Official World*. Dix Hills, NY: General Hall.

Dietary Supplement Health and Education Act. 1994. Public Law 103-417. 103d Congress.

"Dietary supplements." 1998. *Wellness Letter: The Newsletter of Nutrition, Fitness and Stress Management* 14 (11): insert.

"Drug abuse and workplace demographics." 2001. Washington, DC: Office of National Drug Control Policy.

Drug-Free Federal Workplace: Executive Order 12564. 1986. *Federal Register* 51 (180): September 17.

"Drug free workplace." 2002. Washington, DC: Office of National Drug Control Policy.

Drug Testing: A Bad Investment. 1999. Washington, DC: American Civil Liberties Union.

Drug Testing in the Workplace. 1996. Washington, DC: American Civil Liberties Union.

Drug Testing Index. 1999. Teterboro, NJ: Quest Diagnostics. October 19.

Durkheim, Emile. 1893/1933. *The Division of Labor in Society.* Translated by George Simpson. New York: Free Press.

The Economic Costs of Alcohol and Drug Abuse in the United States, 1992. 1992. Washington, DC: National Institute on Drug Abuse.

The Economic Costs of Drug Abuse in the United States, 1992–1998. 2001. Executive Office of the President. Washington, DC: Office of National Drug Control Policy. September.

Ehrenreich, Barbara. 2001. *Nickel and Dimed.* New York: Metropolitan Books.

Engels, Frederick. 1878/1939. *Anti-Duhring.* New York: Free Press.

Fay, John. 1991. *Drug Testing.* Boston: Butterworth-Heinemann.

Ferrell, Jeff. 2001. *Tearing Down the Streets: Adventures in Urban Anarchy.* New York: Palgrave.

Ferrell, Jeff. 1993. *Crimes of Style.* New York: Garland.

"Firms offer ways to foil drug tests." 2003. *Washington Post* February 17: 3A.

Fisk, Milton. 1979. "Dialectic and ontology." Pp. 117–43 in John Mepham and David Hillel-Ruben (eds.), *Issues in Marxist Philosophy.* Sussex, England: Harvester Press.

Fort Worth Star-Telegram. 2002. June 6: 5B.

Foucault, Michel. 1979. *Discipline and Punish.* New York: Vintage.

French, Michael T., C. M. Roebuck, and P. K. Alexandre. 2001. "Illicit drug use, employment, and labor force participation." *Southern Economic Association Journal* 68 (2): 349–68.

Galbraith, John K. 1978. *The New Industrial State* (3d ed.). Boston: Houghton Mifflin.

Garland, David. 2001. *The Culture of Control.* Chicago: University of Chicago Press.

Gieringer, Dale. 1992. "Urinalysis or uromancy? The untold costs of drug testing abuse." Pp. 121–39 in Arnold S. Trebach, Kevin B. Zeese, and Kendra E. Wright (eds.), *Strategies for Change: New Directions in Drug Policy.* Washington, DC: Drug Policy Foundation.

Gilliom, John. 2001. *Overseers of the Poor: Surveillance, Resistance, and the Limits of Privacy.* Chicago: University of Chicago Press.

Gilliom, John. 1994. *Surveillance, Privacy, and the Law.* Ann Arbor: University of Michigan Press.

Glaser, Barney. 1978. *Theoretical Sensitivity.* Mill Valley, CA: Sociology Press.

Glaser, Barney, and Anselm L. Strauss. 1967. *The Discovery of Grounded Theory: Strategies for Qualitative Research.* Chicago: Aldine.

Goffman, Erving. 1961. *Asylums.* New York: Doubleday.

Goffman, Erving. 1959. *The Presentation of Self in Everyday Life.* Garden City, NY: Doubleday.

"Goldenseal: Flower power." 1999. *Wellness Letter: The Newsletter of Nutrition, Fitness and Stress Management* 16 (1): 6–7.

Gomes, Lee, Thomas E. Weber, Don Clark, and Martin Peers. 2000. "Comprehending napster." *Lexington Herald-Leader* July 9: F1, F6.

Goodman, Fred. 2002. "Will fans pay for music online?" *Rolling Stone* January 31: 17–18.

Greenberg, E. 1992. *AMA Survey on Workplace Drug Testing and Drug Abuse Policies.* New York: American Management Association.

Griswold v. Connecticut, 381 U.S. 479 (1965).

Hammersley, Martyn, and Paul Atkinson. 1983. *Ethnography: Principles in Practice.* London: Tavistock.

Hartwell, Tyler D., Paul D. Steele, Michael T. French, and Nathaniel F. Rodman. 1996. "Prevalence of drug testing in the workplace." *Monthly Labor Review* 119 (November): 35–42.

Hartwell, Tyler D., Paul D. Steele, and Nathaniel F. Rodman. 1998. "Workplace alcohol-testing programs: Prevalence and trends." *Monthly Labor Review* 121 (June): 27–34.

Harwood, Henrick. 2000. *Updating Estimates of the Economic Costs of Alcohol Abuse in the United States: Estimates, Update Methods and Data.* Report prepared by The Lewin Group for the National Institute on Alcohol Abuse and Alcoholism. Rockville, MD: U.S. Department of Health and Human Services.

Harwood, Henrick, Douglas Fountain, and Gina Livermore. 1998. *The Economic Costs of Alcohol and Drug Abuse in the United States.* Rockville, MD: U.S. Department of Health and Human Services.

Haynes, V. Dion. 1999. "Illegal pharmacies thriving in some immigrant areas." *Chicago Tribune* March 14: 3.

Hegel, G. W. F. 1807/1931. *The Phenomenology of Mind.* London: Oxford.

Hoffman, Abbie, and Jonathan Silvers. 1987. *Steal This Urine Test.* New York: Penguin Books.

Hubbard, L. Ron. 1990. *Clear Body, Clear Mind.* Los Angeles: Bridge Publications.

"If it ducks like a quack." 1999. *Wellness Letter: The Newsletter of Nutrition, Fitness and Stress Management* 15 (5): 6.

"Implementing a student drug and alcohol testing program." 2002. *DATIA Resources*. July 18. www.datia.org.

Jones v. McKenzie, 628 F. Supp. 1500 (D. D.C. 1986).

"Keeping an eye on ions." 2001. *Wellness Letter: The Newsletter of Nutrition, Fitness and Stress Management* 17 (6): 6.

Kot, Greg. 2001. "What's wrong with radio." *Rolling Stone* August 16: 25–26.

Lewis, Virginia S., Seymour Pollack, David M. Petersen, and Gilbert Geis. 1973. "Nalline and urine tests in narcotics detection: A critical overview." *The International Journal of the Addictions* 8 (1): 163–71.

Lewis, Virginia S., David M. Petersen, Gilbert Geis, and Seymour Pollack. 1972. "Ethical and social-psychological aspects of urinalysis to detect heroin use." *British Journal of Addictions* 67 (4): 303–7.

Lofland, John, and Lyn H. Lofland. 1984. *Analyzing Social Settings* (2d ed.). Belmont, CA: Wadsworth.

Lyman, Michael D., and Gary W. Potter. 1996. *Drugs in Society* (2d ed.). Cincinnati, OH: Anderson.

Lyng, Stephen. 1990. "Edgework: A social psychological analysis of voluntary risk taking." *American Journal of Sociology* 95 (4): 851–86.

Lyon, David. 1994. *The Electronic Eye: The Rise of Surveillance Society.* Minneapolis: University of Minnesota Press.

Marx, Gary T. 1995. "The engineering of social control." Pp. 225–46 in John Hagan and Ruth D. Peterson (eds.), *Crime and Inequality.* Stanford: Stanford University Press.

Marx, Karl. 1867/1906. *Capital.* Volume 1. New York: Random House.

Marx, Karl, and Frederick Engels. 1948. *The Communist Manifesto.* New York: International Publishers.

Massing, Michael. 1998. *The Fix.* Berkeley: University of California Press.

Meikle, Scott. 1979. "Dialectical contradiction and necessity." Pp. 5–35 in John Mepham and David Hillel-Ruben (eds.), *Issues in Marxist Philosophy.* Sussex, England: Harvester Press.

Merton, Robert K. 1938. "Social structure and anomie." *American Sociological Review* 3: 672–82.

Mieczkowski, Thomas M. 1996. "The prevalence of drug use in the United States." Pp. 349–414 in Michael Tonry (ed.), *Crime and Justice: A Review of Research.* Chicago: University of Chicago Press.

Mieczkowski, Tom. 1997. "Hair assays and urinalysis results for juvenile drug offenders." National Institute of Justice Research Preview. Washington, DC: U.S. Department of Justice. Office of Justice Programs. April.

Morgan, John P. 1988. "The 'scientific' justification for urine drug testing." *University of Kansas Law Review* 36: 683–97.

Nakashima, Ellen. 2001. "Group protests drug testing policy." *Washington Post* June 1: A29.

National Drug Control Strategy, FY 2003 Budget Summary, The White House. 2002. Washington, DC: Office of the White House Drug Policy. February.

National Household Survey on Drug Abuse, 2000. 2001. Washington, DC: U.S. Department of Health and Human Services. September.

National Household Survey on Drug Abuse, 1996. 1997. Washington, DC: U.S. Department of Health and Human Services. September.

National Household Survey on Drug Abuse: Highlights 1990. 1990. Rockville, MD: National Institute on Drug Abuse.

National Treasury Employees Union v. William Von Raab, 109 U.S. 1384 (1989).

Nebelkopf, Ethan. 1987. "Herbal therapy in the treatment of drug use." *International Journal of the Addictions* 22 (8): 695–717.

Nebelkopf, Ethan. 1981. *The Herbal Connection.* Orem, UT: BiWorld Publishers.

Nock, Steven L. 1993. *The Costs of Privacy: Surveillance and Reputation in America.* New York: Aldine de Gruyter.

Norman, Richard J. 1976. *Hegel's Phenomenology.* Sussex: Harvester Press.

Normand, Jacques, Richard O. Lempert, and Charles P. O'Brien (eds.). 1994a. *Under the Influence? Drugs and the American Workforce.* Washington, DC: National Academy Press.

Normand, Jacques, R. Lempert, and C. O'Brien. 1994b. "Impact of drug testing programs on productivity." Pp. 215–40 in Jacques Normand, Richard O. Lempert, and Charles P. O'Brien (eds.), *Under the Influence? Drugs and the American Work Force.* Washington, DC: National Academy Press.

Orwell, George. 1949. *1984.* New York: Signet.

Piquero, Alex R., and Stephen G. Tibbetts (eds.). 2002. *Rational Choice and Criminal Behavior.* New York: Routledge.

Potter, Beverly. 1999. *Pass the Test: An Employee Guide to Drug Testing.* Berkeley, CA: Ronin.

"Private high school in Memphis will do drug tests on its entire student body." 2000. *Knoxville News-Sentinel* January 9: B6.

Rasmussen, David W., and Bruce L. Benson. 1994. *The Economic Anatomy of a Drug War.* Lanham, MD: Rowman and Littlefield.

Roe v. Wade, 410 U.S. 113 (1973).

Samuel K. Skinner v. Railway Labor Executives' Association et al., 109 U.S. 1402 (1989).

Sanjek, Roger. 1990. *Fieldnotes: The Makings of Anthropology.* Ithaca, NY: Cornell University Press.

Schwartz, Howard, and Jerry Jacobs. 1979. *Qualitative Sociology.* New York: Free Press.

Shepard, Edward, and Thomas Clifton. 1998. "Drug testing and labor productivity: Estimates applying a production function model." *Working USA* November–December: 1–30.

"Should you believe in magnets?" 1999. *Wellness Letter: The Newsletter of Nutrition, Fitness and Stress Management* 15 (8): 7.

"The skinny on cellulite." 2002. *Wellness Letter: The Newsletter of Nutrition, Fitness and Stress Management* 18 (5): 6–7.

Somerville, John. 1967. *The Philosophy of Marxism: An Exposition.* Minneapolis: Marxist Educational Press.

Sourcebook of Criminal Justice Statistics. 2000. Washington, DC: U.S. Department of Justice.

Stambaugh, J. J. 2002. "Nursing home alarmed by pot tests." *Knoxville News Sentinel* December 17: B-1.

Staples, William G. 1997. *The Culture of Surveillance.* New York: St. Martin's.

"Substance abuse and treatment of adults on probation." 1998. In *Bureau of Justice Statistics.* Washington, DC: National Institute of Justice.

"Supreme Court v. teens." 2002. *Common Sense for Drug Policy.* June 6. www.csdp.org.

Sykes, Gresham, and David Matza. 1957. "Techniques of neutralization: A theory of delinquency." *American Journal of Sociology* 22: 664–70.

Syva Company. 1992. "Frequently asked questions about Syva's Emit drug abuse tests." San Jose, CA: Syva.

Taylor, Frederick W. 1911/1982. *Principles of Scientific Management.* Easton, PA: Hive.

Telecommunications Act of 1996. Public Law 104-104 (S. 652). February 8. 104th Congress, Second Session.

Thoreau, Henry D. 1849/1957. *Civil Disobedience.* Boston: Houghton Mifflin.

Timrots, Anita. 1992. "Fact sheet: Drug testing in the criminal justice system." *Drugs and Crime Data.* Washington, DC: U.S. Department of Justice. Office of Justice Programs. March.

Trebach, Arnold S., and James A. Inciardi. 1993. *Legalize It? Debating American Drug Policy.* Washington, DC: American University Press.

Tsang, Teri. 2003. "Shamed record biz to return public's money." *Rolling Stone* February 20: 8.

Tulacz, Gary J., and Michael P. O'Toole. 1991. *What You Need to Know about Workplace Drug Testing.* Englewood Cliffs, NJ: Macmillan.

Tunnell, Kenneth D. 2002. "The impulsiveness and routinization of decision-making." Pp. 265–78 in Alex Piquero and Stephen G. Tibbetts (eds.), *Rational Choice and Criminal Behavior.* New York: Routledge.

Tunnell, Kenneth D. 1998. "Reflections on crime, criminals, and control in newsmagazine television programs." Pp. 111–22 in Frankie Bailey and

Donna Hale (eds.), *Popular Culture, Crime and Justice*. Belmont, CA: Wadsworth.

Tunnell, Kenneth D. 1992a. *Choosing Crime*. Chicago: Nelson-Hall.

Tunnell, Kenneth D. 1992b. "Film at eleven: Recent developments in the commodification of crime." *Sociological Spectrum* 12: 293–313.

"UFVs: Unidentified funny vitamins." 1999. *Wellness Letter: The Newsletter of Nutrition, Fitness and Stress Management* 15 (9): 8.

United States v. Robert J. Ruiz. 1974. WL 13920 (CMA), 48 C.M.R. 797, 23 USCMA 181.

Vernonia School District 47J v. Acton. 1995. (94-590), 515. Supreme Court of the United States 646.

Wagner, David. 1987. "The new temperance movement and social control at the workplace." *Contemporary Drug Problems* 14 (Winter): 539–56.

Walker, Samuel. 1985. *Sense and Nonsense about Crime*. Monterey, CA: Brooks/Cole.

Wallerstein, Immanuel. 1983. *Historical Capitalism*. London: Verso.

Walliman, Isidor, Howard Rosenbaum, Nicholas Tatis, and George Zito. 1980. "Misreading Weber: The concept of 'Macht.'" *Sociology* 14: 261–75.

Walsh, J. Michael, and Jeanne G. Trumble. 1991. "The politics of drug testing." Pp. 22–49 in Robert H. Coombs and Louis Jolyon West (eds.), *Drug Testing: Issues and Options*. New York: Oxford University Press.

Weber, Max. 1922/1978. *Economy and Society*. Berkeley: University of California Press.

"Wellness facts." 1998. *Wellness Letter: The Newsletter of Nutrition, Fitness and Stress Management* 15 (3): 1.

West, Louis Jolyon, and Deborah L. Ackerman. 1993. "The drug-testing controversy." *Journal of Drug Issues* 23 (4): 579–95.

Whitaker, Aja. 1999. "Tight labor market could mean more drug abuse." *Management Review* October: 4.

Wiese, Jeffrey G., Michael G. Shlipak, and Warren S. Browner. 2000. "Review: The alcohol hangover." *Annals of Internal Medicine* 132 (11): 897–902.

Wild, David. 2002. "Musicians unite against record labels." *Rolling Stone* January 31: 17–18.

Williams, Lance. 1999. "Harlan schools mull employee drug tests." *Lexington Herald-Leader* July 25: A1.

Wilson, Doris James. 2000. "Drug use, testing, and treatment in jails." In *Bureau of Justice Statistics*. Washington, DC: U.S. Department of Justice. May.

Zeese, Kevin B. 1997. *Drug Testing Legal Manual and Practice Aids* (2d ed.). Volumes 1 and 2. St. Paul: West Group.

Zimmer, Lynn, and James B. Jacobs. 1992. "The business of drug testing: Technological innovation and social control." *Contemporary Drug Problems* 19: 1–26.

Index

About the Author

Kenneth D. Tunnell is Professor in the Department of Criminal Justice at Eastern Kentucky University. His previous books include *Living Off Crime* (2000), *Choosing Crime* (1992), and *Political Crime in Contemporary America* (1993). His work has appeared in *Justice Quarterly, Qualitative Sociology, Deviant Behavior, Social Justice,* and *Journal of Popular Culture.*